North Cascades

A Guide to the North Cascades
National Park Service Complex
Washington

SO-AXQ-906

Produced by the
Division of Publications
National Park Service

U.S. Department of the Interior
Washington, D.C. 1986

Using This Handbook
The North Cascades National Park Service Complex includes the north and south units of North Cascades National Park, plus Ross Lake and Lake Chelan National Recreation Areas. Together these lands protect major lakes and the glaciated peaks of the North Cascades mountains. Part 1 of this handbook briefly introduces the park and region. Part 2 explores the park by its two major routes, Highway 20 and the passenger ferry trip up Lake Chelan. Part 3 presents concise travel guide and reference materials.

National Park Handbooks, compact introductions to the great natural and historic places administered by the National Park Service, are published to support the National Park Service's management programs at the parks and to promote understanding and enjoyment of the parks. Each is intended to be informative reading and a useful guide before, during, and after a park visit. More than 100 titles are in print. This is handbook 131.

Part 1

Welcome to the North Cascades

The Pacific Northwest's Mountainous Backbone

Crag-turreted Mount Shuksan defines its own niche on the park's northwest flank. It bears the brunt of the Nooksack, Crystal, Price, and Sulfide Glaciers. Admirers claim Shuksan as North America's most photographed mountain. Difficult to verify, the claim nevertheless befits "The Showpiece of the Cascades." International Boundary surveyor Henry Custer used the Indian name, Tsuskan, when he mapped this peak in 1859. In 1934 The Call of the Wild was filmed here to capitalize on Shuksan as its backdrop.

For Pacific Northwesterners the great outdoors is no mere diversion. It is integral to a lifestyle shaped by their region's astounding natural heritage—rugged seacoast, mountain ranges, dry plateau, tantalizing trout and salmon rivers, and the 300 islands of Puget Sound. Serving as this region's backbone—and some would say protecting its heart as well—is the Cascade Range. And here, just east and north of Seattle, Washington, both region and range culminate in the North Cascades, the jagged, jumbled, snow-capped, and glacier-laden lure for mountain climber, foothills walker, backpacker, and ardent scenery gazer.

If you could mountain-hop inland from the coast, your first two strides would bridge lush forests but leave you face to face with the semi-arid Columbia Basin, Washington's Inland Empire of range lands, irrigated orchards and crop lands, and massive hydroelectric schemes. Behind you would lie the precipitous Northwest Coast and the lush lowlands of the glacier-clad Olympic Mountains, and the spacious Puget Sound trough with its fisheries, refineries, checkerboard farms, and lumber, plywood, paper, and pulp mills.

Lacking such seven-league boots, however, you are more likely to drive up the coast from Seattle, with Puget Sound on your left. Abreast of the San Juan Islands at Burlington, you turn east up the valley of the Skagit River. The wide, coastal floodplain of the Skagit quickly narrows inland, but not before showing you the farms and lumber mills that have been regional economic mainstays. The "sedro" in Sedro Woolley is Spanish for cedar, denoting the forests of western redcedar that once swept down the Cascades' western slopes like gigantic mirror images of the Pacific's crashing surf. Cedar served this region's Indians even more than birchbark served Indians of the North Woods. Large specimens reach 230 feet skyward, outstripped locally only by the Douglas-fir, which may reach 300 feet.

Ponderosa pine dominates the Cascades' eastern slopes, growing up to 175 feet tall. They rise off a forest floor nearly empty of anything but their own litter of twigs and long needles. These forests reflect the radically reduced rainfall east of the Cascade crest. The mountains—first the Olympics and then the North Cascades—have forced inland-bound wet air ever higher, cooling it until it is virtually empty of moisture before reaching these eastern slopes. Although this change by no means appears absolutely abrupt as you cross the North Cascades National Park Service Complex by highway, or as you boat up Lake Chelan, the transition is nevertheless dramatic. Linking as it does the mountains, ocean, and intervening forest splendors, this phenomenon is one of the park's most fundamental ecological revelations, and a major treasure to be preserved.

The North Cascade Range bisects Washington like some ruined wall, and for years few people tried to penetrate this tortuous topography. Early climbers thought the rugged topography would eternally protect itself from exploitation. However, by the 1950s and 1960s, new logging and mining methods threatened to diminish the unique natural features and values that the park would one day be established to preserve.

"The Park was not created without a ruckus," wrote Washington State's late U.S. Senator Henry M. Jackson. He introduced the Senate version of the legislation that eventually created the park. That creation came in 1968, but the ruckus began way back in 1892, when Chelan townspeople issued the first call for a national park in the North Cascades. They were upset over the slaughter of mountain goats and grizzly bears by Eastern and European sportsmen. In 1897, just five years after this first proposal, more people actually lived in the North Cascades than have ever lived here before or since. These were miners, however, and the very next year most of them pulled up stakes and trekked north to join the great Klondike Gold Rush in Alaska. Many of these small-scale sculptors of the landscape probably found Alaska's rigors relatively routine by comparison with this overwhelming alpine terrain, where lowcountry and highcountry are so inextricably mixed that "roughcountry" becomes the best description.

Gunsight Notch dwarfs climbers on the Ptarmigan Traverse, a popular route that begins at the park's Cascade Pass. The scale of the North Cascades, massive and geologically tempestuous, diminishes only with sufficient distance and the ubiquitous haze. The Cascade Range stretches from the Fraser River in British Columbia south into California, reaching its highest elevations in northern Washington. Its glacially sculpted peaks and pinnacles, severe and dramatic, are unmatched in the contiguous 48 states.

A North Cascades Panorama

The tortuous complexity of the North Cascades Range, one of North America's most rugged landscapes, is dramatically depicted in this panorama by Heinrich Berann of Lans, Austria. From a vantage point above the range's crest you are looking westward across the Pacific Northwest outdoor recreation mecca. The view descends the Skagit River Valley and across Puget Sound and the Strait of Juan de Fuca to the Olympic Peninsula and to Victoria, British Columbia, Canada. The airline distance from Stehekin, near the head of Lake Chelan at the middle left, to Ross Lake at the Canadian border, lower right, is about 50 miles. From Mount Baker to Glacier Peak and to Mount Rainier the distances are 55 and 132 miles, respectively. A poster version of this panorama is available from the park association at the address shown on page 89.

Mount Rainier

Glacier Peak

SEATTLE

LAKE CHELAN

STEHEKIN

Stehekin River

Thunder Creek

Granite Creek

North Cascades Highway

Peaks and Passes

1 Dome Peak
2 Mount Formidable
3 Johannesburg Mountain
4 Cascade Pass
5 Sahale Mountain
6 Eldorado Peak
7 Boston Peak
8 Buckner Mountain
9 Booker Mountain
10 Goode Mountain
11 Easy Pass
12 Rainy Pass
13 Washington Pass
14 Liberty Bell Mountain
15 Ruby Mountain
16 Colonial Peak
17 Pyramid Peak
18 Mount Triumph
19 Bacon Peak
20 Mount Shuksan
21 Mount Challenger
22 Mount Prophet
23 Sourdough Mountain
24 Jack Mountain
25 Desolation Peak
26 Hozomeen Mountain

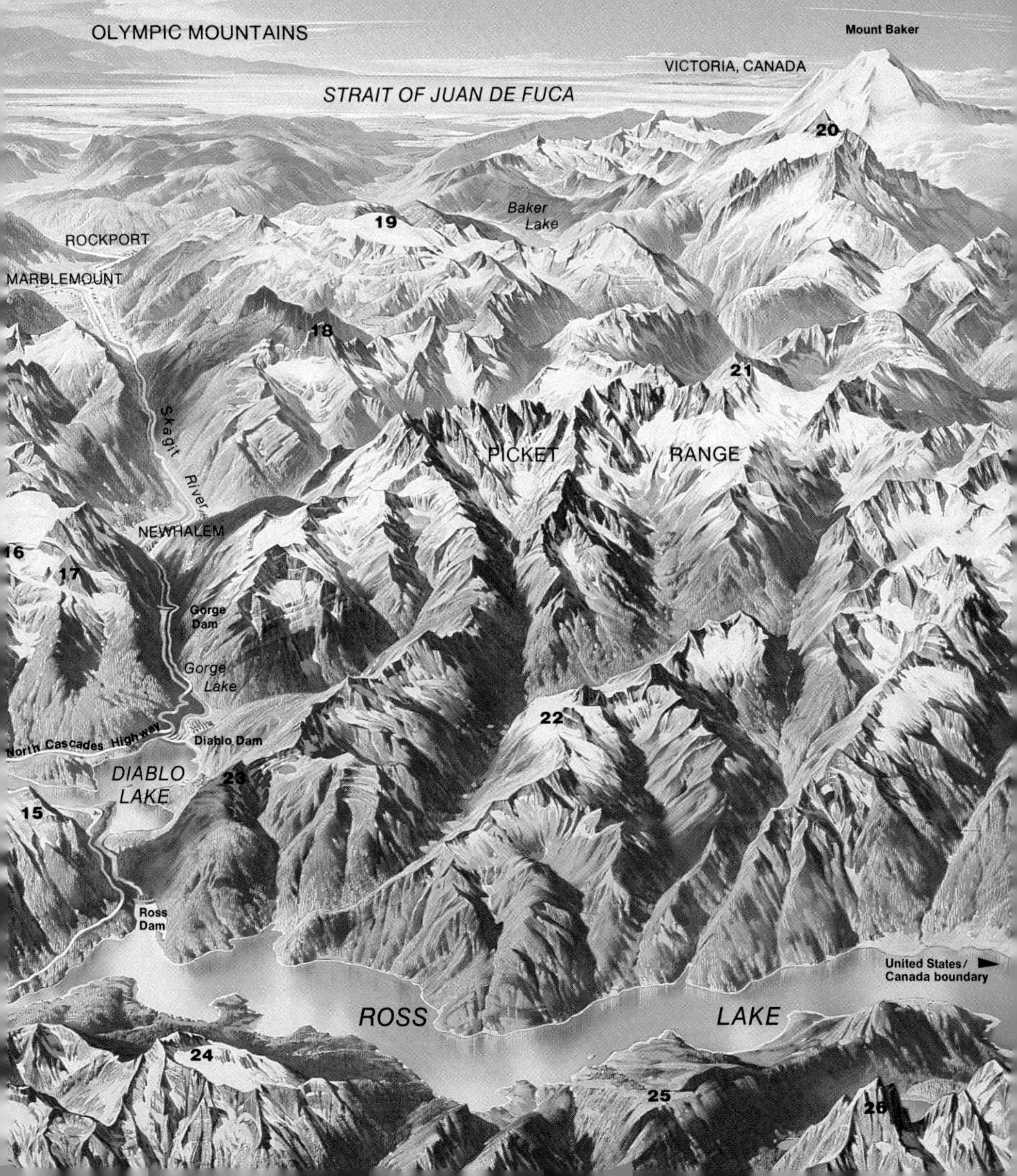

OLYMPIC MOUNTAINS
Mount Baker
VICTORIA, CANADA
STRAIT OF JUAN DE FUCA
20
19
Baker Lake
ROCKPORT
MARBLEMOUNT
18
21
Skagit River
PICKET RANGE
NEWHALEM
16
17
Gorge Dam
Gorge Lake
22
North Cascades Highway
Diablo Dam
DIABLO LAKE
23
15
Ross Dam
United States/ Canada boundary
ROSS LAKE
24
25
26

Climbers on the Challenger Glacier enjoy a visual illusion that recreates the effect of the Ice Age. Mounts Baker and Shuksan jut above the clouds. Mount Challenger, due north of Highway 20 at Newhalem, rises to 8,248 feet elevation. It lies in the North Cascades National Park's north unit. Shuksan—see page 6—rises 9,131 feet. Volcanic Mount Baker, just west of the park in Mount Baker-Snoqualmie National Forest, reaches 10,775 feet.

Roads remain a rarity here, and access continues to be most practical on foot. And so it is that in the North Cascades the backpacker has found what the miner could not: that ever elusive Eldorado.

Besides witnessing a one-time population explosion here, the year 1897 also saw President Grover Cleveland create the Washington Forest Reserve. Eventually these lands became the Mount Baker, Wenatchee, and Okanogan National Forests. The park was created from these lands by their transfer to the National Park Service in 1968. From 1892 to the 1960s, national park proposals for the North Cascades occurred at the rate of about one per decade. Unanimity among the many concerned interest groups—timber, mining, hydroelectric, hunting, real estate, conservationists, environmentalists, alpinists, backpackers, and more—eluded the park's architects. However, public sentiment favored dedicating these lands as a complex of a national park and two national recreation areas.

The North Cascades—the mountains themselves and all they imply—are the primary attraction. They are the culmination of the great Cascade Range that runs from Northern California's volcanic Lassen Peak all the way into Canada. To the south the Cascade Range is often a vast, high plateau whose profile is only periodically punctuated by jutting, isolated volcanic peaks. But here an unbridled chaos of alpine peaks juts skyward in close formation. The North Cascades, which are not volcanic in origin, begin at Stevens Pass east of Seattle and stretch on to their geological terminus in British Columbia's Manning Provincial Park.

Before the European discovery of the Americas, today's park and its surroundings were the domain of some 10 Salishan-speaking peoples. West of today's park were the Skagit, Samish, Lummi, Nooksack, and Semiahmoo; to the east were the Okanogan, Methow, Chelan, and Wenatchee; and to the north were the Thompsons. These mountains were so severe that none of these people lived here year-round. They traveled here in summer for hunting, fishing, and gathering, and for transmountain commerce. To many of these early residents these mountains were, although not eternal, divine. Their collective memories encompassed incidents of peak-destroying volcanism that ruled out calling them eternal. These peaks were the realm of the gods. They included places forbidden to mortals on pain of misfortune or destruction.

To the explorers in the late 19th century, such stupendous mountain scenery was, if not eternal, at least esthetically sublime and spiritual. Images of eternity were often used in the early attempts to describe the North Cascades. They are also present in much subsequent mountain climbing literature. Yet it is the shortness of human memory and history that contributes this illusion of mountain eternities.

The image of unassailability that early climbers thought would protect the North Cascades from exploitation ignores the alpine fragility inherent in these high places. Because of the climatic extremes, nutrient-poor environments, short growing seasons, and island-like characters, mountains exhibit a vulnerability and inability to recover from damage. Alpine and subalpine vegetations require protection from undue human impact. But the mountains themselves are preserved for their impact on us. The imagery and collective memory that untouched mountain realms evoke must, here and there, be protected so that they are not everywhere lost, and with them the plants, animals, and mini-environments unique to mountains. The 1968 decision designated the North Cascades just such a protected mountain realm.

Monarchs of the craggy heights, mountain goats roam realms that would give roped-up alpinists pause. Both sexes have horns, unlike Dall sheep, with whom mountain goats are often confused. But Dall, mountain, and bighorn sheep do not live in the park, so you won't be confused here. Mountain goats are sure-footed, cautious, and deliberate. Their almost square hooves combine a rigid outer edge with soft, almost rubbery inner pad. They are psychologically disposed against panic; under threat they calmly and deliberately walk away.

*Western redcedars (left) pro-
vided materials for clothing,
lodging, and transportation
for Pacific Northwest In-
dians. All but a few of these
once numerous and vast forests of redcedars have been
logged off.*

*The Cascade Range derives
its name from countless
waterfalls tumbling off its
peaks. Their numbers pre-
clude the naming of many of
them. This waterfall, in Lake
Chelan National Recreation
Area, enlivens a creek that
flows into Lake Chelan.*

Pages 18-19. *Glacier-laden
peaks peer above the head of
Stehekin Valley, seen here
from Stehekin Landing on
Lake Chelan. From the left
are distant Sahale Mountain,
and Boston, Booker, and
Buckner. The Cascade Pass
Trail threads just west of
Sahale, reaching an elevation
of 5,384 feet at Cascade Pass.*

Pages 20-21. *Forest floors on
the range's western slopes
also exhibit some of the complexity characterizing jumbled alpine realms above.*

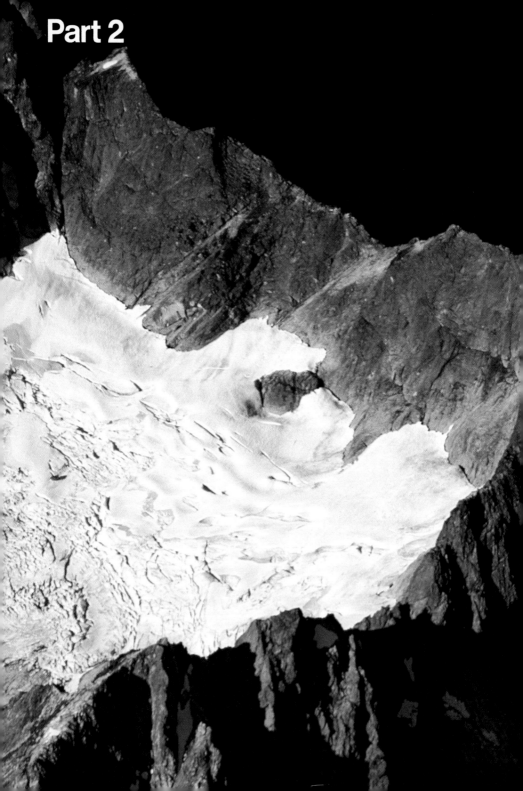

Part 2

Two Passages to Wildness

The North Cascades Highway

Pyramid Peak, rising 7,182 feet, looms above a bend in Highway 20, the North Cascades Highway. Transmountain road proposals fueled the dreams of early fur traders and a succession of miners, loggers, and others eager to exploit the region's natural wealth and recreation potential. The North Cascades Highway, the first road to bisect the range north of Stevens Pass, was opened in 1970. Winter snow and avalanche danger close it to through traffic. Part of it has been named the North Cascades Highway Scenic Area.

On clear days—a qualifying phrase heard often in these mountains—the North Cascades beckon you eastward as you drive along Interstate 5 between Seattle and Vancouver, British Columbia. The range exerts its inland pull despite the manifold coastal delights of "The Other Washington." Its distant snow-capped peaks evoke little surprise: sights of Mounts Hood, Rainier, Baker, and Olympus and the Canadian Rockies punctuate Pacific Northwest travel. The sharpness—the severity—of the North Cascades does stand out, however. The sheer, jumbled profusion of mountains is compelling.

You and I know this corner of the United States as the Pacific Northwest, but geologists call it Cascadia. The Cascade Range of mountains made an early impression on these matter-of-fact scientists. This geologic scenario is probably less understood than any similar-sized chunk of North America. Even offshore this geologic region is one of the world's most difficult to understand. And everyone, including the Indians, got a late start learning about this geological jumble of peaks and pinnacles.

Bacon Creek crosses Highway 20 on the park's southwest edge at just 330 feet above sea level. Just to the northeast, Damnation Peak stands more than 1 mile above sea level. Vertical changes happen abruptly here. As an Oregonian in the Newhalem Campground exclaimed, "You can sunburn your tonsils looking at the scenery!"

At the western edge of Ross Lake National Recreation Area, Highway 20 hugs rock faces—the flanks of the mountains—above the Skagit River. The rock faces display vignette after vignette of mosses and small evergreens, like myriad large-scale Bonsai gardens. Now and then the road opens onto flats where weathered stumps suggest former forest splendors, while against the road shoulders a profusion of plants raises a wall of green as if to hide the secret vistas beyond. At Goodell Creek Campground redcedars, moss-encrusted forest behemoths, rise beside the Skagit River. It would require a whole family's linked, outstretched arms to grasp their true girth. Mosses cling to convoluted bark ridges and declivities. These are worlds within worlds, each the gift of time and the plentiful coastal rains. You need only a mental frame, superimposed from scene to scene, to create your own masterpieces of memory.

When you leave the campground, what you missed on the way in now catches your breath—a peek at the towering Picket Range. The sculpted realm of snow and ice sits like a stage set above a curtain wall of evergreens. Don't miss this Pickets preview. You will get very few such glimpses of the alpine backcountry from Highway 20.

Above Newhalem and the Seattle City Light enclave, Highway 20 hints at where it is leading you—into a deep gorge. Cascades of rushing water, some of the myriad waterfalls for which the range is named, make reckless leaps off near-vertical gorge walls, seeking sea level.

At Gorge Creek, above the highway, two ravens bask in a cold cascade mist atop a jagged boulder. The boulder eventually will fall to the gorge floor far below. Stream pounding, rolling, and tumbling may then reduce it to the workable raw materials of future soils—perhaps. Another scenario might be: A cataclysm could recycle it directly back to Earth magma. These mountains are second cousins to that recently erupted volcano, Mount St. Helens. Insulated against the cascade's chilly shower, the two ravens sit stock still, mere micro-blinks in Earth time.

Through shifting cloud veils higher up the gorge walls, bleached tree spars materialize now and then, looking at first glimpse like other plunging cascades. Sloping rock ledges are greened with mosses thick enough to turn a climber's cleats into virtual downhill skis. Anything loose falls dramatically. With angles so set, gravity judges swiftly in these valleys.

Henry Custer, an American topographer surveying the international boundary in 1859, got a taste of gravity's swift rule here. Up in the highcountry and intrigued by the phenomenon of pink snow, Custer and his partner decide to return to camp. "We found by near inspection that the descent from this plateau where we stood, & which forms the divide, to the

Creek bottom was over 3000 ft.," he wrote, "& from its almost perpendicular inclination almost unpracticable." They risked it and survived, but as Custer observed, "Once to have lost foot hold here, nothing would have been left only to the unlucky climber but to resign himself to the inevitable fate of being dashed to pieces on the sharp & frightful rocks below him."

A goodly number of mountain peaks here were named by mountain climbers, not by surveyors. Hence, with the Damnation mentioned earlier, such names as Challenger, Desolation, Forbidden, Fury, Terror, and Redoubt abound. Being close to heaven has its hazards.

Custer's 47-page report still reads well today, with its awe for the character of these mountain wilds: "To ascend a Mt in the easiest & best way is just as much a matter of good judgment as anything else. The following rules should guide travelers in the Mts. If starting from the foot of a Range or System of Mts, you wish to penetrate to its Interior, always select the largest stream arising in this Range or System of Mts in the vicinity and follow its course."

That is precisely what you do on Highway 20, tracking the Skagit River until veering off at Ross Lake's Ruby Arm, bound for Granite Creek and Rainy and Washington Passes. Until Highway 20 opened in 1972, no road bridged the North Cascades between Stevens Pass, Washington, and the Hope-Princeton Highway in Canada, an alpine span of 90 airline miles. This testifies to the formidable mountain barrier, not to any lack of determination of the succession of traders, miners, loggers, and others who from Custer's time forward periodically sought to push through one transmountain route or another. Even today the road is closed much of the year by snow, ice, and avalanches.

One park ranger, whom we will call George Mullen, is a former logger who knew this country long before the road pushed through. He conducts a campfire program about the history of logging in the North Cascades. The program concludes with an appeal to preserve one of his great loves, the western redcedar. Sixty or 70 campers of all ages are gathered in the Colonial Creek Campground amphitheater. It is almost dark as George quits the security of the amphitheater podium and jumps up on the only

A kayaker does an "endo" on the Skagit River. River runners can put in near Goodell Creek campground (see map inside front cover). From there upstream to Gorge Dam, extreme fluctuations in the water level make conditions too hazardous.

Pages 28-29. *The Skagit rushes through Skagit Gorge, but the river has been tamed. Three dams on the river supply hydroelectric power for Seattle. The river and its three impoundments form the core of Ross Lake National Recreation Area.*

Pages 30-31. *Ross Lake was created by Ross Dam, the highest and farthest upstream of the Skagit Power Project dams. Highway 20 briefly skirts the south shore and Ruby Arm of this long, north-south trending lake. At Ross Lake Overlook you can perceive the extent of the lake's clear, blue waters. In contrast, Diablo Lake appears bright green, because its waters are colored by fine rock sediments pulverized by glaciers. Far fewer glaciers feed Ross Lake.*

Skagit Hydroelectric Power Projects

Water rights hunters invaded the Cascades just after 1900. The early days were rife with promoters, but only governments and big utility companies would harness the Skagit's power. Seattle City Light grew out of the utility that first harnessed the Cedar River for drinking water and to light the city's streets. As rivalry with Puget Sound Power and Light escalated,

Seattle City Light decided to dam the stupendous Skagit gorges above Marblemount. The old Gorge Dam was completed in 1924, Diablo Dam (shown below) in 1930, and Ross Dam in 1949. The new Gorge Dam was completed in 1960. Their turbines can generate a combined 786 megawatts of electricity, enough to supply one-third of Seattle's peak demand. Access for construction equipment and supplies was a problem. After first exploring roadbuilding, the company

built a 22-mile railroad line from Rockport to Diablo. Construction delays caused by forest fires, washouts, labor unrest, and lack of electricity doubled the original estimated cost of Gorge Dam. The first organized tour of the Skagit Power Project, for the Seattle City Women's Club, was conducted in 1928 by the project's tireless booster, City Light head James D. Ross. See Part 3 for today's tour information.

Dam	Height	Maxium lake depth of dam
Gorge	300 feet	140 feet
Diablo	389	354
Ross	540	460

vacant spot on the front row of bench seats.

"You may think it's funny that I, a park ranger, am going to tell you about the 'glory days of logging' here in these mountains," he begins. "But I hope when we're through you'll see that this is an appeal to save some very special trees."

A tall man whose considerable strength focuses on his upper body, George immediately commands a quieting attention from his audience. He holds up a weathered and work-worn pair of logger's overalls: "I also want to answer two questions many people have: 'Why do loggers wear suspenders,' and 'Why do loggers chew snoose?'"

George grew up in these woods, down in the Skagit Valley, just across the river from the town of Rockport. Town after town has come and gone here since the heyday of logging. Some still exist as names even though their communities have long since disappeared.

"My family got into other ventures from time to time," he says, "but we always returned to the woods for a living. We always got back to logging to get by."

He holds up the large-toothed crosscut saw and asks if anybody knows what it's called.

"Misery whip!" comes the cry from half-way back in the amphitheater.

"Well I better be careful what I say tonight," George exclaims, "there's at least one logger in the crowd!"

He explains what a springboard is, thumps it into place on the demonstration tree stump, and jumps up on it to attack the stump with a double-bitted ax. The chips begin to fly clear to the front row. Given the apparent precariousness and uncertainty of the bouncing springboard perch, the precision bite of George's ax seems uncanny.

"I'm not saying we shouldn't cut any more trees. I'm just saying that there are some we ought to save." He calls his campfire program on logging "The Last Stand."

It is the western redcedar that George is impassioned to save. This grand tree once served the economic needs of Native Americans in this locale much the same way that birchbark did those in the northeastern and northcentral states. It was the primary resource for their material culture, from clothing to transportation. Its straight, tight grain and weathering characteristics make this cedar ideal for shakes. Every town along the river used to have a shingle mill for cutting shingles from shingle bolts—split cedar blocks—that were floated down from bolt camps on up the rivers.

George's amphitheater audience includes, among many others, a family from New York State, some folks from North Carolina, and a few residents of the lower Skagit Valley. Some have been boating and fishing on Diablo Lake and its Thunder Arm today. Others have been enjoying campground life. Still others spent the previous night in the backcountry, near Fourth of July Pass on a ridge that has now become the faintest of silhouettes behind the amphitheater. George doesn't forget to answer his own two questions: Loggers wear suspenders because you have to be able to move inside these heavy overalls, and you don't want to be bound at the waist. Loggers chew snoose (dip snuff) because they need their hands free, they don't want smoke in their eyes, and they want no more flame or glowing embers in the woods than are needed to get the job done.

The program ends with a woman from the audience volunteering to rive off a redcedar shake with mallet and froe. She hefts a mean mallet and rives a respectable tapered shake, and the amphitheater crowd gives her a rousing cheer.

On Highway 20 you are in Ross Lake National Recreation Area. Nowhere does the highway enter North Cascades National Park. Throughout most of the park complex, once you leave the road, or the lakes, there are few perceptible differences. The North Cascades' claims to wildness are more a matter of character than classification. The virgin stand of the redcedars that George Mullen loves best is found in the Big Beaver Creek Valley, on Ross Lake's west shore. Draining a part of the Picket Range, Big Beaver Creek flows out of the north unit of the national park and into the recreation area.

Ross Lake's east shore is somewhat less wild than its west shore, if only because a trail runs its length. Nevertheless, the east shore has its share of wild places. Not the least of these are Jack Mountain, Desolation Peak, and Hozomeen Mountain. Hozomeen is such an awesome presence that many climbing books just call it Hozomeen, without prefix or suffix. After a summer at the cabin on Desolation Peak,

Logging Days

Loggers began to harvest the North Cascades' forest bounty in the 1860s, beginning with low-elevation valleys. Much of today's park area was never commercially logged. Elevation, ruggedness, and inaccessibility protected it. From the park west to Puget Sound lumbering was a major economic activity. The *sedro* in Sedro Woolley means cedar in the Spanish language and recalls the western redcedar's importance in early lumbering. At first, ox teams hauled logs to the river on skid roads greased with, among other things, fish oil. Trees were felled with axes, later replaced with crosscut saws, then chain saws, and finally heavy mechanical cutters. The early loggers came up the Skagit and cut trees without regard to land ownership. By 1883, land along the Skagit had been mostly claimed. Loggers either cut trees they owned or paid stump fees. The Skagit's first logging railroad was built in 1882 at Burlington. The first mill capable of producing machine-sawed shingles was built in 1886 at Sedro. The steam donkey, invented in California in 1882, began to replace oxen along the Skagit by 1884. This device—steaming in the photograph—wound in logs by a cable rolled on a

large drum. The line was at first hauled back out by horses, but they were replaced by a second drum arrangement about 1900. About 1915, the date of this picture taken on the Skagit near Concrete, loggers began to bring the logs in on high leads rather than drag them flat across the ground. The steam donkey disappeared as gasoline- or diesel-powered equipment was adopted in the 1920s and 1930s. And roads were built for hauling logs out by chain-drive trucks. These heavy-laden early trucks were, according to some loggers, "aimed, not driven;" note the wheels on this truck. The lower Stehekin Valley was also logged. Methods were the same, but the delivery system differed. Steamboats hauled rafts of logs down Lake Chelan to Chelan mills.

Western redcedar

Grows to 230 feet.
Trunks have natural
buttresses.

Douglas-fir

Grows to 300 feet.
Most common conifer
west of Cascades.

Ponderosa pine

Grows to 175 feet.
Has distinctively long
needles.

Western larch

Grows to 260 feet.
Its needles turn gold in autumn,
then drop.

Forest Fire Lookouts

Forest fire surveillance is accomplished by satellites and aircraft today. When the era of forest fire lookouts ended in the 1960s, Washington State boasted more than 500 lookout stations. Many were in today's park. The first lookouts began work in this region about 1910. They merely climbed a high point in summer for a look around. Then tent sites with sighting instruments were used, followed by cabins in more strategic locations. During World War II women donned uniforms to watch for fires, and many Pacific Northwest lookouts doubled as aircraft spotting positions. During lightning storms—when the lookout was to be particularly on duty—the lookout's cabin might sustain numerous strikes. Lookouts

sat on stools with electric insulators on the legs. The late Beat novelist Jack Kerouac's lookout stint on the park's Desolation Peak is recounted in *Desolation Angels*. Pulitzer Prize-winning poet Gary Snyder's lookout stint on Sourdough Mountain (inset photo) is recorded in numerous poems and the prose collection, *Earth House Hold*. The large photo shows the Copper Lookout, on Copper Mountain in the park's extreme northwest corner.

one fire lookout described Hozomeen as an "awful vaulty blue smokebody rock."

A teacher from Bellingham, Washington, whom we will call Alan Paulson, figures he has chalked up more than 600 trail miles in the North Cascades. Right now he is balanced on a sharply sloping rocky point spin-fishing. He throws spinners after trout at a mountain lake within sight of Hozomeen. A traditional Indian might blame the spirits of Hozomeen for Alan's lack of angling success today. Alan himself has seen so much of the North Cascades backcountry over the past 10 years that maybe he, too, blames the mountain for his bad luck. Alan is trying to carry on an intelligent conversation with another backpacker who has just stumbled into his picturesque backcountry campsite. The conversation suffers on two counts. Alan's thought patterns keep getting short-circuited by the sound of trout breaking the water's surface. Each rise jerks his head automatically toward its audible dimpling. This unseats his precariously situated feet, which then start sliding toward the lake surface just below. Alan suffers a low grade case of Izaak Waltonism, trying to cast his spinner into one widening set of concentric circles after another.

"Are you sure you want to catch a trout? You'll have to cook it," Alan's companion offers.

"The sound of trout rising drives me crazy," Alan admits. "I call it my 'Uncooked Melody.'"

That sounds like a "Yes" answer.

The second conversational problem is also environmental. A sound keeps reaching up and over the lake from an undetermined direction. It falls somewhere between a muffled bear growl and a bullfrog croak. It is one of those inscrutable backcountry noises that reverberates in your head, one of those few noises that increases as you get farther from civilization.

In fact, a bear sow and her cub have been very active at this campsite recently, according to the backcountry rangers at Ross Lake's north end. This reality is not lost on Alan and his friend. They recount many bear stories from their collective pasts. Alan draws a distinction between terrified and bear-ified.

"I refuse to worry about bears," he asserts. Nevertheless, the inscrutable sound wafting over the lake's

A cyclist replenishes liquids on the North Cascades Highway. The seemingly endless climb to the highway's summit is everywhere rewarded by unmatched mountain scenery.

Pages 44-45. *The gamut of alpine scenic attractions greets you in the short distance between Rainy and Washington Passes. Coniferous forests, subalpine meadows, picturesque mountain lakes, and great piles of rock, or scree, unfold in rapid succession. Crowning these delights are Liberty Bell Mountain (foreground) and the Early Winter Spires, seen from Washington Pass. East of the pass you immediately descend into dry landscapes.*

The Range Divides Washington State

The Cascade Range's tall mountains force wet, eastward-moving air ever higher, cooling it until it looses its moisture as precipitation. The almost rain forest conditions west of the range are contrasted on the east by semi-arid foothills. West of the range are two major forest types, the western

Annual precipitation 80 inches at Newhalem west of the range.

1 Mountain hemlock
2 Alaska yellow cedar
3 Subalpine fir

4 Pacific silver fir

5 Western hemlock
6 Douglas-fir
7 Western redcedar

46

hemlock and Pacific silver fir. East of the range you find open sage and ponderosa pine communities, which require far less moisture. Forests of the west side stand in lush underbrush, but Ponderosa pine forests stand in the parched litter of twigs and needles they drop. By shielding the interior from moisture-laden Pacific winds, the Cascade Range divides Washington State into two distinct regions.

Annual precipitation 34 inches at Stehekin east of the range.

8 White bark pine
9 Alpine larch
10 Subalpine fir

11 Lodgepole pine

12 Ponderosa pine

Fragile Mountain Plantlife

The conditions of life on high mountains are rigorous. Wind, cold, excessive sunshine, sparse soils, and extremely short growing seasons test survival. Most plants have adapted structurally. Alpine counterparts of familiar plants are usually much smaller. This minimizes wind exposure as they lie close to the ground, where it is often several degrees warmer than just a hand's height above. Many grow in matted configurations, massed low to the ground for wind and cold protection. Many have hairy stems and waxy leaves to protect them against cold and against moisture loss from constant high winds. Despite low temperatures, too much sun also proves a problem. Some healthy alpine plants are red-brown or brown in color. These dark pigments protect them from certain solar rays the atmosphere cannot adequately block at these high elevations.

The blossoms of alpine plants may be exaggerated in scale, looking far too large for their stems and leaves. This adaptation helps attract pollinators during the brief period available for reproduction. And many are pollinated by flies and spiders, not bees, whose blood freezes at higher temperatures. Seed-bearing plants must be able to blossom and be pollinated within several days, not weeks. Damage done to such fragile eco-

Plants and animals of the mountain world:

1 Redtail hawk
2 Pika
3 Hoary marmot
4 Cushion buckwheat
5 Whitebark pine

6 Alpine fir krummolz
7 Heather
8 Dwarf willow
9 Pixie-cup lichen
10 Grey-crowned rosy finch

systems can take hundreds of years to repair naturally. Unfortunately, such delicate meadows and passes are popular highcountry spots. Some have been over-used until worn down to bare ground. At some mountain passes you may find jute netting (inset photo) covering trail scars and protecting seedling transplants. The National Park Service, Student Conservation Association volunteers, and other volunteer workers have been growing alpine plants in a greenhouse built by Young Adult Conservation Corps workers at the Marblemount Ranger Station. The seedlings are backpacked to abused areas for transplanting in this successful revegetation project.

11 Alpine forget-me-not
12 Moss campion
13 Alpine phlox
14 Haircap moss

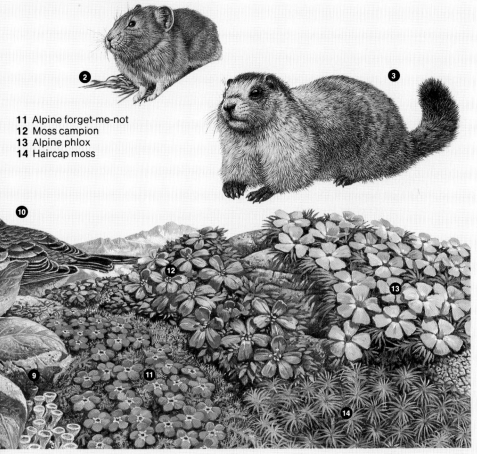

surface persists in stopping his conversation cold.

"What does that sound like?" He repeats for the umpteenth time. He doesn't miss a cast, however.

Observed with detachment, the behavior of the miners who ranged over this region during the 1858 Fraser River Gold Rush and well into the 20th century proves only slightly less singleminded than that of the most committed angler. Miners erected small towns in mountain reaches where today's backpackers might fear to tread. An ingenious group these miners could be, too, as the saga of Happy Creek exemplifies.

Happy Creek crosses Highway 20 at Happy Flat, near the Ross Dam Trail parking area. Start down this dry trail and you quickly hit the air-conditioned coolness of the creek. The Seattle City Light Department has altered Happy Creek's course so that it now comes out above Ross Dam, thereby adding economic value to Ross Lake hydropower. But the miners went one better. They harnessed Happy Creek way up on Ruby Mountain, using its hydropower to saw timber for a wooden flume. Then the miners floated lumber via the flume to Ruby townsite where it was used for buildings and to divert water from Ruby Creek so they could work the streambed. Ruby townsite now lies below today's Ruby Arm of Ross Lake.

Mining activity in what is now the park did not pick up momentum until 1880. The Fraser River Gold Rush that began in 1858 prompted the boundary work that topographer Henry Custer participated in, however. Americans had wanted routes into Canada that avoided British assessments for access to the fields. Mining activity in the park area continued into the 1950s. Many mining claims and patents still exist within the park, although the National Park Service has acquired many since the park's creation. Strikes were negligible, overall. Most profits came not from mining but from the sale of claims to other, more optimistic parties. Access, and the difficulty of reaching markets, proved limiting factors for marginal mining operations. The miners did speed settlement of the North Cascades, however, and they provided impetus for numerous transmountain road plans and projects.

Cultural values sometimes shift rapidly. As you crest the Cascade Range on Highway 20, first at

Rainy Pass and then at Washington Pass, you are struck by the spectacular high-mountain scenery. Yet what attracts us to Cascadia's backbone today is what repulsed the Indians, traders, miners, and settlers even into our own century. Their worst obstacles have become our opportunities for enjoying the natural scene. We now choose to enjoy the whole, rather than to exploit some of its parts. Today, the remarkable behavior here belongs not to surveyors, miners, or loggers, but to backpackers and alpinists. Some of their choicest destinations and challenges are briefly glimpsed from the road, but their exploits cannot be. The wilderness that prevails within mere steps of the road surface exists on far too grand a scale to permit such ease of surveillance.

WILDFLOWERS

Shooting star

Fireweed

Bunchberry

Avalanche lily

Mountain heather

Wild lupine

Indian paintbrush

Columbine

Cow parsnip

Avalanche fawn lily

Foxglove

Alpine phlox

Orange agoseris

Trillium

Pleated gentian

Red monkey flower

WILD ANIMALS

Mountain goat

Bald eagles

Cottontail rabbit

Blacktail fawn

Douglas squirrel

Raccoon

Marmot

Ptarmigan

Western tanager

Porcupine

Columbia blacktail deer

Mallard hen

Osprey

Black bear

Red fox kit

Pika

Stehekin: The Way Through

The Wapato Indian word chelan *means deep water. Did these early residents understand just how deep Lake Chelan is? Sonar measurements place its depth at 1,528 feet. Its deepest point lies 426 feet below sea level. Lake Chelan, at 50.4 miles long, averages about 1 mile in width.*

History takes on a palpable, tactile quality at Stehekin. The passenger ferry journey— a large boat on a large inland lake—smacks of historic transport. At Stehekin Landing you look up the road that deadends in the valley, unconnected to the outside world of roads. If you consider the whole history of human settlement in the heart of the North Cascades, the Stehekin Valley was a veritable beehive. But the bees were grounded; outside the hive they could only walk. No roads pass into or out of Stehekin. And so, a historic lifestyle continues uninterrupted here in Lake Chelan National Recreation Area. The mix of private and park lands preserves a way of life not linked by road to 20th-century life. Valley residents conduct their commerce with the "outside" via ferryboat. They order groceries by letter with a blank check enclosed. The supermarket fills and boxes the order and drops it off at the ferry dock in Chelan. Next stop: Stehekin Landing. Substitutions for out-of-stock items demand culinary ingenuity. Items too bulky or too heavy for ferry shipment—building materials or maybe a pickup truck—travel on the infrequent freight barge.

Fur trading Canadian entrepreneur Alexander Ross was the first European known to have crossed the Cascade crest, via the Twisp River and Copper Pass. He pushed on up the upper Stehekin Valley and across Cascade Pass in search of beaver and sites to promote the Northwest Company's fur trapping business. His last Indian guide, fearing supernatural reprisal for having trespassed on the realm of the gods, finally deserted Ross because of a fierce storm that struck shortly after they reached the Skagit River. Meet a fierce storm yourself in this rugged wilderness and you may side with the Indian, not Ross. Ross himself turned back short of Puget Sound. The year was 1814. Stehekin would have to wait some 60 years to earn its place on the maps, little more than a decade before the American frontier was pronounced officially closed.

Alexander Ross was not really blazing a trail. Rather he followed Indians across the mountains on a route they had used for years. Of the primitive Cascades transmountain routes, Cascade Pass was the most used. It narrowly missed selection for both road and railroad routes. In the end no transportation route crossed Cascade Pass before its recognition as prime backcountry reserved it for footprints only. Ross' trail became the Cascade Wagon Road, parts of which exist today, sited generally above the present valley road; but the road was not to cross the pass.

Alexander Ross would have loved the route you take today to Stehekin Landing. The excitement begins at dockside as travelers eagerly await the morning's boarding of a steel-hulled, diesel-driven passenger ferry. You glide at 14-knots into history, and beyond—the Indian word "Stehekin" roughly translates as "the way through." For many this marks a personal passage that transcends time.

At the start of the trip, boarding begins a rush for seats inside or on the upper or lower open decks, depending on the weather and your preference. Once settled, you take in the details of the boat and then your attention shifts to the lake and its encircling mountains. For the next few hours, to the tune of surging diesels, you have but two environments, that of the boat and that of mountain-encircled Lake Chelan. The voyage seems longer than its actual hours because it is a journey of years, perhaps 50 years, into the past. It's a classic approach to the North Cascades, and a rare travel treat.

The lakeshore's lower portion is given over to a drier aspect frequently interrupted by homes. These then become more sparse until finally only an occasional vacation dwelling snuggles to the lakeshore. From aboard, the shore scene appears like a model railroad layout, although, despite its 50-mile length, Lake Chelan's width rarely exceeds 1 mile. As you ply its length, this glacier-carved fjord seems more like a wide river than a lake.

There are picturesque stops en route, although you do not disembark if Stehekin is your destination. The boat puts in at Lucerne, an apt name for a townsite on a fjord, and at Moore. Holden Village rests high above Lucerne, out of sight up the Railroad Creek valley. Holden Village operated as a mine until 1957. In 1961 the mining company donated it to the Lutheran Church, and it is now a religious retreat community. Holden is also a popular jumping-off point for backpacking trips through the Glacier Peak Wilderness and into the park.

There are sometimes unscheduled stops. The passenger ferry has been known to carry such incidentals as salt licks for deer at the behest of the Washington State game agency. Such stops are another firsthand glimpse of history, for this boat and her predecessors have traditionally served as lifelines for communities up and down the lake.

You are not long afloat before your interest perhaps turns inward, from the scenery to other passengers. What is their ultimate destination? What will they do there? Where are they coming from? The passage uplake often creates camaraderie, so the best way to satisfy your curiosity is to ask. Some people's garb gives immediate clues to their intentions. Backpackers, depending on the weather, may sport heavy lug-soled hiking boots and wool socks exposed by short pants. Their moods may shift quickly as their focus shifts from talking to gazing out at the mountains rising ever farther above as you progress up the lake.

A crew member periodically uses the public address system to tell you something of the scenery you are passing, about the lake's creation and depth, or about local lore. In recent years the state released mountain goats from Olympic National Park on Lake Chelan's shores in an effort to re-establish this species here. Keep your eyes peeled. A mountain lion sometimes is spotted from the water, but this is unfortunately rare. You could be lucky; a pride of several of these cougars was once spotted cavorting along the Lakeshore Trail.

By now the Cascades loom above you, bespeaking their own rough wildness as they also wall the horizon far beyond the lake's head. Your destination, Stehekin Landing, will shortly be in view.

At Stehekin Landing you claim your baggage as you disembark. Chances are an unprepossessing park ranger whom we will call William Carroll will be helping to speed the offloading. The backcountry is permanently imprinted on this quiet man. There is a lightness to the set of his frame, a distinct lift to his gait. That gait had its genesis in the backcountry,

The First Lady of the Lake

The *Belle of Chelan* was launched on Lake Chelan in 1889, commencing year-round boat services that continue to this day. The early boats were slow-moving craft that burned prodigious quantities of wood as fuel. What they lacked in speed, some boats, such as the *Stehekin*, made up for in elegance. As the *Chelan Leader* newspaper reported in 1900: "The steamer Stehekin, is 'a thing of beauty and a joy.' In addition to a commodious ladies' cabin there has been added a gentleman's smoking room and a galley, the one forward and the latter aft of the cabin. A number one range and all the other accoutrements of a well furnished kitchen have been put in place, and regular meals will be furnished the passengers hereafter. The ladies' cabin is furnished with a grand piano, sofa and easy chairs. The pilot house has been placed above the cabin. On the lower deck is ample room for all the freight business likely." Two other craft that were the match of the *Stehekin* in size and comfort were operated on the lake by 1900.

These were the *Swan* and the first *Lady of the Lake*. The first *Lady*, a steam boat, is shown here hauling apples on Lake Chelan about 1900. To the people who lived uplake the boats were a lifeline. They depended on them for supplying both physical and cultural needs. The same holds true today, but with a difference. Whereas in the early years the boats functioned to push away for a few moments the vast wilderness of the Cascades, today more people push into that wilderness via the boats than use them as lifelines for daily living. For a time during the heyday of transcontinental railroad travel, Lake Chelan's boats provided the final transportation link between Stehekin's hotels and most major municipalities in the United States. The steamboat whistles have now been replaced by electrical air horns. Today's *Lady* and her sister boats are powered by diesel engines.

Scenes from the *Lady's* Passage Today

The skipper at the helm

The lower lake's dry slopes

The view from shore

Refreshments aboard

Destination: backpacking

Anticipation

Isolated cabins onshore

Other modes of lake travel

Disembarking at Stehekin

Stehekin Landing, and Up the Valley Road

Anglers off the docks

And anglers on the docks

Groceries arrive by boat

Some valley residents

Horses at Courtney Ranch

Kayaking Stehekin River

64

Backpackers adjust loads

North Cascades Lodge

Road's end

Lake Chelan Dips Below Sea Level

Lake Chelan is the largest natural lake in Washington, third deepest in the United States, and seventh deepest in the world. It is 50.4 miles long and averages about 1 mile wide.

The lake basin's deepest part lies 1,528 feet below the surface—and some 426 feet below sea level. Gigantic glaciers gouged out this great trough 15,000 to 20,000 years ago. A gravel moraine pushed up by the Okanogan Lobe of continental glaciation forms the lake's natural dam. The lake's natural level elevation is 1,079 feet. A dam built in 1927 raised the lake surface to 1,100 feet.

This hydroelectric dam draws the lake down toward its pre-1927 natural level in winter. Some 48 streams and one river, the Stehekin, empty into Lake Chelan. Its water is so pure that its resulting low nutrient content provides little food for fish. Much of their food comes right off the shoreline. Today's anglers vie for rainbow trout, kokanee ("silvers") salmon, and chinook salmon, mostly by trolling.

Shaping the Mountain Scene

Persistent sculpting by glaciers of the range's unusually hard rock created today's fantastic mountain scenery.

Continental Glaciation. The Ice Age began some 2 million years ago and ended 10,000 to 12,000 years ago. Successive ice sheets blanketed the northern continents until glaciers covered 30 percent of the Earth's land surface. (The figure stands at 10 percent today.) In North America these continental ice sheets pushed south as far as Montana, Illinois, and New Jersey, striking even further south along mountain systems. The ice sheets were more than a mile thick; only the tallest peaks protruded above the ice here. Protruding peaks are called nunataks. The photograph on page 12 of mountains jutting above the clouds suggests the Ice Age scene here. Continental glaciation gouged out Lake Chelan Valley to a depth of 1,500 feet.

Mountain Glaciers. A Little Ice Age 3,000 years ago built today's mountain glaciers. There are 318 in the park. Glaciers form where perpetual snow exists. Light snowflakes compress to a granular mass, which further compacts as accumulating weight presses

Horn-shaped peak

Col

U-shaped valley profile

the air out. Gravity causes the resulting ice mass to flow downhill as a relentless river of ice. Its center flows faster than its sides, which meet more resistance from the landscape. Flow rates can vary from an inch per day up to yards. Glaciers stabilize when their rates of snow accumulation and snowmelt equalize. When climate cools, the glacier front advances until a new equilibrium is reached. If climate warms, the glacier then retreats. Glacier ice both scours and plucks the land surface. A mountain glacier will gouge out a bowl-shaped amphitheater called a **cirque**. Two cirques that meet will be separated by an **arête** (literally "fish bone"), a sharp ridge. The convergence of three cirques forms a **horn-shaped peak**. Where cirques break through each other, a saddle-like **col** forms. Lakes created in cirques are called **tarns**. Glaciers gouge streamcut, V-shaped valleys into a **U-shaped profile**. Where smaller, side glaciers enter a valley, the lower, larger glacier's deeper cut may give rise to hanging waterfalls.

and you will wish you possessed it the first time you face a half-day's steady climb up steeply graded or switchbacking trails.

The backcountry surrounds you at Stehekin Landing. "I could talk about this country all day," William says. "It's what I like to do." He worked these mountains with trail crews for seven years before the park's creation. It was national forest land then, and he worked with the U.S. Forest Service before donning his National Park Service uniform. Working on a trail crew in those days was somewhat different than it is today.

"We went out all summer," he recounts. "We'd start out low on the southern exposures as soon as the trails were clear of snow. Then we worked our way up to higher elevations with the snowmelt and descended as winter chased us down and then out of the mountains." Having built and maintained his share of trails, William has profound respect for them, but he knows their limitations, too.

"The real gems of places here, the highcountry gems, are not found on the trails. Trails are built where it's practical to put a trail. They're not built for the most beautiful spots. Many of those are alpine lakes. Some don't have regular trails to them, but you can find them."

William's own favored backcountry methodology is to backpack every other day, day-hiking out of his campsite on alternate days.

"That way you can get off the trails to some of the really beautiful places with just a day pack and your camera or fishing gear. It's not so hard as packing every day," he counsels. "You enjoy it more."

There are countless options for visiting Stehekin, but three are most common. Many folks go up for the day on the ferry, returning after a one-and-a-half-hour layover. Others stay at the North Cascades Lodge for about two days. The folks William has been talking about will stay three or more days for backcountry camping or backpacking. The park staff, concessioner, and some residents offer a variety of services, facilities, and programs to enhance your time here. These are outlined in the Stehekin section of Part 3.

Stehekin offers perhaps the most convenient threshhold to prime backcountry in the National Park System. Shuttle buses ply the valley road between Stehekin Landing and Cottonwood Camp (see map). Nearby lies the magnificent Glacier Peak Wilderness Area of Mount Baker National Forest. By linking up with the Pacific Crest National Scenic Trail, the truly adventurous can backpack into Canada, or all the way to Mexico via the crests of the Cascade Range and the Sierra.

The quality and extent of the backcountry speaks for itself. Across from the lodge, Castle Rock shoots skyward right from lake level. Peeking through the "V" of the valley's distant head are Sahale Mountain and the three Bs—Boston, Booker, and Buckner. Buckner prominently wears the Buckner Glacier, hinting at the short summer in the highcountry. The backside of Boston Peak bears the immense Boston Glacier, which confirms the short summer for those still skeptical.

For the ardent and trail-wise backpacker, linking up the shuttle bus system and the ferry boat with the backcountry opens up magnificent loop-trip opportunities on either side of the lake. This eliminates the problem of ferrying cars or exchanging keys at some halfway point with another group of backpackers.

The campsites that lie near the valley road provide ideal situations for families wishing to ease their way into wilderness backpacking. With the benefit of the shuttle bus to tote your gear in, you can give your outfit a test run under simulated backcountry conditions. You can get used to mechanics of camp life without private vehicle access. You can try the family out on backcountry trails with day hikes of various lengths and difficulties, right from your campsite. Some campsites offer loop-trip opportunities for day trips, saving you from backtracking.

There is a deceptive domesticity to the Stehekin Valley environment. It is difficult to imagine, particularly in summer, that this cozy valley once stood under gargantuan mantles of ice that serrated the peaks and gouged out the Lake Chelan trough so deep that it reaches down below sea level. You can't see the hardships of the early human settlement days. What remains has been softened by nature. A romantic quality suggests itself—at the Buckner place, for example. You are too much in the woods here to know that just up the valley stand fields of perennial snow on horizons of more knife-edged peaks than you will find anywhere else in the Lower

Stehekin Homesteading Days

Just three miles up the valley from Stehekin Landing, the Buckner place exemplifies the earliest homesteading here. The large photo shows the Buckner barn that is no longer standing and the inset photo shows the Buckner Cabin, which features rough-sawn boards and a fieldstone fireplace. The cabin was built of logs by William Buzzard in 1889, with an addition built later. The ingenuity and self-sufficiency demanded by this pioneering lifestyle are revealed in the many tools and implements preserved in the homestead structures (see following pages). The Buckners operated this property as a self-sufficient homestead from 1911 to 1953. Major ingredients for their

success, besides ingenuity, were copious amounts of hard work, knowledge of natural processes, and some good luck. Park rangers conduct daily walks through the old Buckner place during the summer season. These walks— and the rangers' narratives— recapture a sense of this once pervasive way of life that has largely vanished from the American landscape.

Traces of the Homesteading Lifestyle

A hard-won clearing endures

The cabin's original logs

1929 Fordson tractor

1932 Ford truck

Chains—ready for use

Tools in the work shed

74

An abandoned wagon

Barrels by the shop

Listening to the world

The Era of Grand Hotels

The first hotel on upper Lake Chelan was built in 1889 on Moore's Point by New Yorker James Robert Moore. The vacationers shown in the inset photo are seated on its porch about 1900. Begun in 1900, the famous Field Hotel (large photo) could accommodate 100 guests by 1910. It replaced the smaller Argonaut Hotel that M. E. Field bought from George Hall in 1892. The earliest hotels served the mining trade, but the miners' tales of stupendous scenery soon attracted tourists. The Field Hotel boasted acetylene gas lighting with chandeliers in the ballroom. In 1916 the Great Northern Railroad bought the Field Hotel, running package tours to it from most U.S. points. You could book ferry passage uplake on a weekend, dance all night, and return (snoozing to the boilers' roar?) on the next day's downlake ferry. When Lake Chelan's level was to be raised, the Field Hotel was torn down be-

cause it stood below the projected new lake level. Much of the salvage, including interior trim, parts of the staircase, and the fireplace were used in 1927 to build the Golden West Lodge, which operated until 1971. Today the Golden West Lodge is the National Park Service visitor center at Stehekin. Other hotels here included Rainbow Lodge and the Purple House—named for its owners, not its color.

The Black Warrior Mine

Albert Pershall and M. M. Kingman located the Blue Devil and Black Warrior claims in beautiful Horseshoe Basin in 1891. This period saw copious promising gossip of gold up in the rugged wilderness peaks. Pershall and Kingman sold their claims for $30,000 cash, sparking the mining boom for gold, silver, copper, lead, and zinc. The prime target was galena, a silver-lead ore that usually contained gold. The boom bordered on hysteria: There was talk of tunneling 4 miles under the basin's pinnacles to connect with mines in the Thunder Creek drainage, and of building a railroad up Lake Chelan. This heady optimism died out by the beginning of World War I, but new interest in mining Horseshoe Basin, whose elevation is 6,000 feet, was sparked by shortages of copper, lead, and zinc after World War II. A mine-to-market road was built up from Lake Chelan. Most of the equipment found at the mine today dates from this era.

Investigation of these claims again in the late 1960s found no commerical ore. One winter at the Black Warrior Mine (shown here in the 1940s) the miners traveled back and forth to the mine shaft from their cabin via a 50-foot tunnel through snow. Dangers were present from the rugged terrain and from mining practices. Avalanches and rockslides were frequent hazards, Blasting caps ignited in the blacksmith shop here in 1899. The two men present were blown clear outside, and the shop was destroyed. One man died of his injuries despite a doctor's efforts down at the head of Lake Chelan. The remains of the Black Warrior Mine are open to the public now. You can reach this location by a 2.5-mile hike from the last shuttle bus stop, at Cottonwood Camp.

Mining's Heyday

Most of the money made from mining in these parts came from the sale of claims to others more optimistic about their fortunes. The spectacular mountain scenery we enjoy today made for difficult mining logistics. Most mines failed to produce ores of high enough grades to make their operations pay. In the second half of the 19th century, however, vast numbers of miners came to the Cascade mountains and valleys. The influx began in the Stehekin Valley in the 1880s. The earliest hotels in the Stehekin Valley served the mining trade almost exclusively. Mostly these people found the dreams they pursued and little else. As you step off the Park Service shuttle bus at Bridge Creek, popu-

lation zero, it is difficult to imagine that its population was once reported as 2,000. Those were the mining days. The confluence of Bridge Creek and the Stehekin River was a local staging point for prospectors and miners. The photograph shows an assay office either in Bridge Creek in 1892 or at Meadow Creek in 1893. The pile of rocks at the opening of the assay office tent (right) is ore samples. Note the fancy trim of the tent at left. While miners made the area boom only briefly, they set the stage for tourism by talking up the wonders of Lake Chelan and Stehekin's superb scenery.

Lucky the North Cascades traveler who sets eyes on the reclusive mountain lion. These great cats do inhabit these wilds, however, and you may be among the lucky few. Scan Lake Chelan's shorelines through your binoculars. A pride of seven mountain lions once crossed a footbridge on the Lakeshore Trail in full view of surprised ferry passengers. While mountain goats are native to the North Cascades, the recent transplant of goats along Lake Chelan may improve the lot of the mountain lion.

48 states. Flat land is at a premium—no, it is a rarity—in these parts. The Buckner place is one of those rare valley flats.

An Iowan whom we will call Gordon James has returned to Stehekin for several summers now to work for the National Park Service. After giving his passengers an orientation at Stehekin Landing, Gordon has taken them via a Park Service shuttle bus to Stehekin School, where he reviews the history of this quaint log structure.

Then he guides the group over Rainbow Creek to the Buckner place. Because we will be walking single-file, he explains, we will have to pause now and then and circle up to talk about what we're seeing. Our way begins through shaded woods, alongside a picturesque irrigation ditch. The wooden flume gives way to a raised rock mini-aqueduct, a work of ingenuity, if not genius. Your imagination seems to flow with it into the Buckner place, pulling you into the Stehekin Valley's pioneering past.

The Buckner place began as a 160-acre homestead developed by prospector Bill Buzzard, who came to the valley in 1889, wearing his black fedora—complete with bullet hole. Buzzard sold out to William Van Buckner, the younger brother of Henry Freeland Buckner. Freeland was Buzzard's prospecting and carpentering contemporary, for whom Buckner Peak is named. William Van's son, Harry, came to the place in 1911 and remained the rest of his life, except for his World War I military service.

Gordon calls a group halt as we emerge from the woods alongside the irrigation stream. Here a massive cable is rigged to a geared wheel set on a frame flat to the ground.

"What's this," he asks?

"That's a stump puller just like my granddaddy used on his place," someone volunteers.

"Yes," Gordon confirms, with a smile. "I especially enjoy leading this walk when there are folks along who get a chance to relive childhood farm experiences. This is the Hercules stump puller the Buckners used to clear their land."

Gordon helps a youngster gear the cable for putting pressure on the tree at its opposite end. Even with a mule, uprooting the tree would be no easy task.

Though the apple packing shed is now just a concrete slab, many of the Buckners' apple trees are still bearing and in good shape. You can pick and eat an old variety of apple no longer grown commercially, Gordon explains. The community will gather here in fall and press out apple cider, but the community must share these apples, too—with Stehekin's bears! Bears regularly put the Buckner orchard on their autumnal itineraries, as do the deer. Our nature walk temporarily disperses as we fan out through the orchard, searching for the perfect apple to pick.

The Buckner Cabin lies across the farm road from the orchard. Built by William Buzzard in 1889, it goes back nearly to the beginning of Stehekin's settlement history. He added a board-and-batten section to the log cabin in 1910, and interior renovations took place up into the 1940s. According to Harry Buckner, they built the fireplace and chimney in 1911.

The Buckners kept a couple of pigs, about eight cows, and some young beef stock for hams, milk, and roast beef. The worst job—or so the Buckner children thought—was cleaning the cream separators. Excess cream might be sold to Stehekin tourist lodges, perhaps by boat delivery.

It being warm, but not uncommonly so for Stehekin in August, Gordon invites us to step into the root cellar, an above-ground structure insulated by its sawdust-filled walls and thick door. Once we are all crowded inside with the door shut, he points out the obvious. It is not only cool, but also pitch dark and smelling of apples.

The Buckners' new home, built during the farm's later years, now houses a park employee and his family. We sip cider served up by his wife, who fields our questions: What is it like living like this? How do you feel about your children walking to school with bears around? Is this cider from the orchard? She graciously answers each question as though we were the first to ask it.

Our farm tour nears its end, and Gordon is not content to leave us without an enigma to ponder. Down by the Buckners' swimming pool he points out the stand of large trees. Their large size says they pre-date the pool's construction.

"Why did they build the swimming pool in the shade?"

After much inconclusive and unsatisfactory speculation—it was too hot; they were allergic to the sun; as post-Victorians they were too modest—we give up and ask for the answer.

"I don't know," he says. "As far as I know, nobody knows."

We cross a field to the shuttle bus for the two-mile ride back to Stehekin Landing. Everyone is silent now, taking last looks at the Buckner spread. That "nobody knows" seems to echo among us, subtly framing our just-completed journey into Stehekin's pioneer past. We begin to see why they say the valley road begins at the ferry landing and deadends in paradise.

Part 3

Guide and Adviser

Approaching
the North Cascades

The North Cascades National Park Service Complex is composed of three units: a mountain wilderness national park and two lake-based national recreation areas. The National Park Service manages this complex as two districts, the Skagit District and the Stehekin District. For purposes of planning your trip and your time here, the Skagit District is that area reached by and from Highway 20. The Stehekin District is that area reached by traveling up Lake Chelan, typically by passenger ferry. The only other mechanized access to the park complex is at the north end of Ross Lake in the Skagit District (see map), by gravel road from Hope, British Columbia, Canada. An array of backcountry trails gives access to the park complex from adjacent public lands.

Highway 20 and the Cascades Loop In 1972 Highway 20 was opened and for the first time people could travel across the North Cascades in a vehicle. Highway 20 is also known as the North Cascades Highway, and is acknowledged as one of the most beautiful mountain highways in the country. The section from Ross Lake National Recreation Area's west boundary to near Early Winters has been designated by Congress as the North Cascades Highway Scenic Area. Throughout, the road threads a stupendous landscape of mountains, gorges, and lakes. Highway 20 provides access to the park's Skagit District, including Gorge and Diablo Lakes and trails to Ross Lake, and to the trails that lead into the backcountry reaches of both the north and the south units of the national park. From Highway 20 at Marblemount, the Cascade River Road leads up to the Cascade Pass Trailhead. Highway 20 also provides the northern arc of the Cascades Loop.

The Cascades Loop The Cascades Loop comprises a seashore to mountains and sagelands network of roads circling from Seattle north to Burlington, then east to Winthrop, south to Chelan and Wenatchee, and west back to Seattle. For information on the loop and its many recreation possibilities, request a Washington State Highway Map from the Transportation Administration Building, Olympia, WA 98504, (206) 753-2150; and literature from the Cascade Loop Association, P.O. Box 3245, Wenatchee, WA 98801, (509) 662-3888. Washington State also offers travel counseling. From within the state call (206) 753-5600; otherwise toll free (800) 541-9274. At Chelan, reached by Routes 2 and 97, you can charter a float plane or catch the passenger ferry up Lake Chelan to Stehekin Landing. See the Stehekin section below for information on activities, facilities, and services there.

Nearby National Park Areas If you are approaching the North Cascades from the east, via Interstate 90 and Spokane, you may include Coulee Dam National Recreation Area, Box 37, Coulee Dam, WA 99116, (509) 633-0881, on your itinerary. The Cascades Loop and/or I-90 and I-5 along Puget Sound put you within range of Mount Rainier National Park, Tahoma Woods, Star Route, Ashford, WA 98304, (206) 569-2211; the Olympic Peninsula and Olympic National Park, 600 East Park Avenue, Port Angeles, WA 98362, (206) 452-4501; Puget Sound and the San Juan Island National Historical Park, P.O. Box 429, Friday Harbor,

WA 98250, (206) 378-2240, and Ebey's Landing National Historical Reserve, Box 774, 23 Front Street, Coupeville, WA 98239. The Washington State Ferries, Colman Dock, Seattle, WA 98104, (206) 464-6400, provide ferry service across Puget Sound and to the San Juan Islands. This service is vital for anyone traveling from Seattle to Olympic National Park or to San Juan Island National Historical Park.

The Highway 20 Corridor

Information Centers Information may be obtained at park headquarters, 2105 Highway 20, Sedro Woolley. As of this writing a new location is planned for the main visitor center in the park. Inquire at park headquarters for current information about the visitor center. Information and backcountry permits can be obtained at the **Marblemount Ranger Station**, 1 mile north of Highway 20 just east of Marblemount (see map). Exhibits here portray mountain climbing, safety, and mountain rescue. A relief model of the park shows the North Cascade mountains in detail. Maps, climbing guides, and other publications can be bought here. A bulletin board lists current trail and climbing conditions, and comments from returned parties. Even if you do not plan backcountry travel, a visit here gives you vicarious experience with the off-road North Cascades wilds. In a small greenhouse here alpine plants are grown for revegetating places in mountain meadows and passes where the plants have been trampled so much that only bare ground remains.

How to Use Your Guide and Adviser

The pages that follow present separate facilities, services, and activities information for the Highway 20 Corridor and for the Lake Chelan/Stehekin area. General information on fishing, backcountry use, mountain climbing, safety, and park management appears after the Stehekin information.

The shaded relief depiction of the park's mountains on the map (pages 90-91) shows how Highway 20 threads a deep gorge. Because of this you will want to stop at the overlooks for glimpses of the vast alpine wonders beyond the gorge walls. Panoramist Heinrich Berann's interpretation of the North Cascades (cover and pages 10-11) presents an aerial perspective of the range in its Pacific Northwest setting. Overlooks are labled on the map and described on pages 92-93. The map's colors distinguish park lands from other public lands adjacent to them. These colors also distinguish the two national recreation area units from the north and south units of the national park.

For information about the park, write to the Superintendent, North Cascades National Park, 2105 Highway 20, Sedro Woolley, WA 98284. Telephone (206) 856-5700.

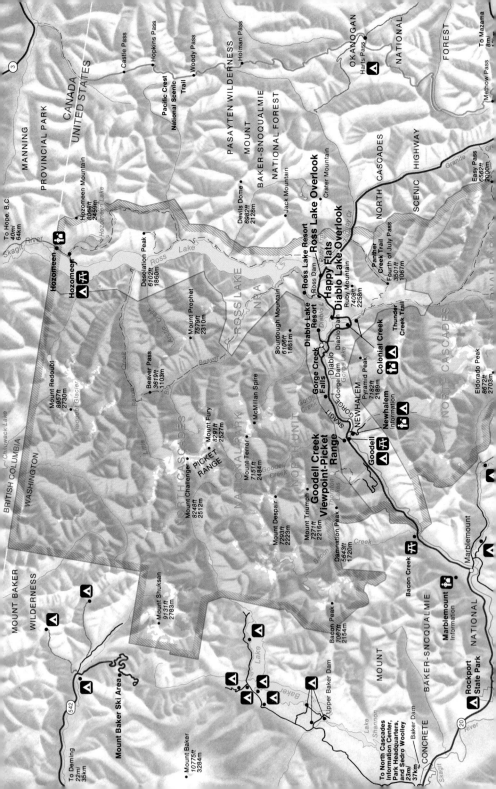

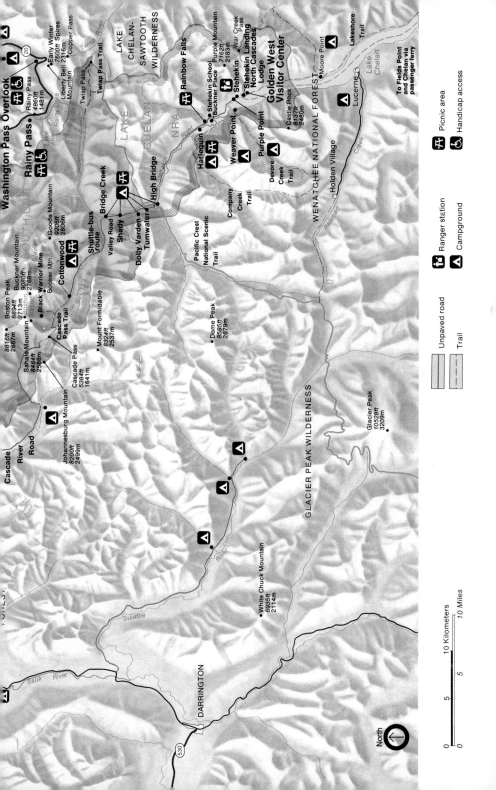

Washington Pass Overlook

Rainy Pass
4860ft
1481m

Rainy Pass
4860ft
1481m

Early Winter
Spires 7600ft 2316m
Liberty Bell
Mountain 7808ft 2316m
Copper Pass

Twisp Pass

Twisp Pass Trail

LAKE
CHELAN-
SAWTOOTH
WILDERNESS

LAKE

CHELAN

NRA

Rainbow Falls

Stehekin School
Buckner Place
Stehekin
Purple Mountain
7162ft
2183m
War Creek
Pass

Stehekin Landing
North Cascades
Lodge

Golden West
Visitor Center

Moore Point

Lakeshore
Trail

Lake
Chelan

Harlequin

Weaver Point

Purple Point

Castle Rock
8137ft
2480m

Devore
Creek
Trail

Lucerne

To Fields Point
and Chelan via
passenger ferry

Holden Village

WENATCHEE NATIONAL FOREST

Company
Creek
Trail

Railroad

Bridge Creek

High Bridge

Shuttle-bus
route

Shady
Dolly Varden
Tumwater

Valley Road

Cottonwood

Goode Mountain
9206ft
2806m

Booker Mtn
Black Warrior Mine

Buckner Mountain
9080ft
2768m

Boston Peak
8894ft
2713m

Sahale Mountain
8484ft
2558m

Cascade
Pass Trail

Cascade Pass
5384ft
1641m

Mount Formidable
8324ft
2537m

Pacific Crest
National Scenic
Trail

Dome Peak
8695ft
2679m

GLACIER PEAK WILDERNESS

Glacier Peak
10528ft
3209m

Boston River

Johannesburg Mountain
8200ft
2499m

Cascade
River
Road

8816ft
2687m

FOREST

White Chuck Mountain
6935ft
2114m

Suiattle
River

Sauk River

DARRINGTON

530

North

0   5   10 Kilometers
0   5   10 Miles

Unpaved road

Trail

Picnic area

Handicap access

Ranger station

Campground

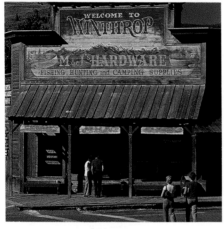

Watch for the North Cascades Information Center on Highway 20 at Sedro Woolley, Washington, west of the park. Displays show sightseeing and recreation options in this area. Books, maps, and posters of the North Cascades may be purchased here and information about nearby public lands is also available.

Winthrop, Washington (bottom photo), awaits travelers east of the park. The Old West flavor this hardware store captures is no quirk. The entire town delivers a delightful time warp. Shops and sundry establishments purvey the full range of merchandise.

Across from the information center are the administrative offices for the park's Skagit District.

Naturalist Programs Naturalist programs are conducted daily from mid-June through Labor Day at Newhalem and Colonial Creek Campgrounds. These include naturalist-led walks and hikes, and illustrated evening campfire programs. The walks and hikes explore various aspects of the North Cascades' natural history, from banana slugs to tarns (small mountain lakes). The campfire programs explore the park's history, prehistory, natural history, and wilderness values and activities. Weekly schedules of these programs are posted in campgrounds and at information centers. **Hozomeen Campground Programs** Naturalist-led walks, hikes, and evening campfire programs also are conducted at Hozomeen Campground, at Ross Lake's north end. This campground is accessible by trail or boat from Highway 20; otherwise you must use the gravel road south out of Hope, British Columbia. A self-guiding nature trail here takes you along the international boundary, just a few paces up the road from the park entrance station.

Activities

Overlooks The scenic overlooks at Gorge Creek Falls, Diablo Lake, and Ross Lake should be integral parts of your park experience. These are the vantage points from which to capture the sense of the astounding mountain peaks that surround you. The road lies in the depths of the Skagit Gorge, whose high steep walls effectively hide the mountains from you. Do not pass by these overlooks. Even on windy, rainy days you won't want to miss the mountain-and-lake scenery of a lifetime that they provide. Wayside exhibits explain many natural features and creatures that you may see. After you leave the east boundary of the Ross Lake recreation area, **Rainy Pass** offers short hikes to Lake Ann and Rainy Lake (wheelchair access). The view at the overlook at Rainy Lake is well worth the 1-mile trip. **Washington Pass Overlook** offers a breathtaking glimpse of Liberty Bell Mountain and the Early Winter Spires, as well as the grand, looping bend of Highway 20 far, far below you. The ample parking at overlooks also provides a chance to get out of the car, stretch your legs, and give the driver a break from the rigors of mountain driving. This area is accessible to those in wheelchairs.

Short Walks and Day Hikes The park's more than 300 miles of trails provide numerous possibilities for short walks and day hikes along the Highway 20 corridor. Campgrounds serve as starting points for **Self-Guiding Nature Trails**. Many offer booklets that explain natural and scenic features you encounter en route. These trails provide excellent limbering-up experiences and new understandings of the natural world. They are short, easy, and pleasant introductions to the North Cascades.

For customized advice on walks and short hikes, stop at an information center or campground office and talk to the ranger. Describe your aspirations and physical condition. He or she can prescribe the trail for you. To make such requests by mail before your visit, write to the park. Even on the shortest hikes in these mountains, you must be prepared and equipped for bad weather. The weather can change from glorious to threatening with great suddenness; you simply can't see what's happening beyond the

ridges that rise so abruptly beside you. Be wary of fording streams. Footlogs and bridges cross most larger streams, but if you must ford, use a long, stout stick as a third leg. If you are wearing a pack, undo its waiststrap—you might have to jettison it if you fall. *Please remember that any overnight use of the backcountry requires a free backcountry permit.*

Horse Use For information on horse use, see Backcountry Basics.

Picnicking Picnic areas are shown on the park folder map. There are also picnic areas for public use on the Seattle City Light grounds in Newhalem. Please leave your picnic area as clean or cleaner than you find it.

Boating and Floating In the Highway 20 corridor, most boating takes place on Diablo and Ross Lakes. There is vehicular access to **Diablo Lake** at the Colonial Creek Campground, with a launch facility, ample parking and turn-around space, and a fish-cleaning station. You also can boat on Diablo Lake as a guest at Diablo Lake Resort (see Accommodations). By advance arrangements with Ross Lake Resort (see Accommodations), you can have your hand-portable boat or canoe trucked over the private service road for launching on **Ross Lake**. Otherwise, the only vehicular access to Ross Lake is at its north end, via the gravel road out of Hope, British Columbia. Another alternative is to carry your boat or canoe down the Ross Dam Trail (see map) by hand, a difficult feat on this steep trail even for those in good physical condition. Or you can rent a boat from Ross Lake Resort. Such arrangements must be made in advance because, for all practical purposes, you cannot reach Ross Lake Resort except by boat or on foot.

Despite these complicated logistics,

Abundant rainfall west of the range waters wildflowers beside Marblemount Ranger Station and lush forests along Thunder Creek Trail (middle photo), above Diablo Lake. Park interpreters share the why of such things with young children.

let it be said that boating on Ross Lake can open up vast wilderness experiences for the adventurous. The boat-in campgrounds spaced along the lakeshore make ideal temporary retreats from the pressures of modern life. For a list of these boat-in campgrounds (free backcountry permit required), write to the park. You can arrange with Ross Lake Resort to be ferried with your gear to lakeshore campsites. Camping is restricted to these designated camps. (For another boating option, see Skagit Tours below.)

Boating Regulations and Safety Federal and state boating regulations are enforced on all waters in the national park complex. Remember to check your boating gear before you leave home. Approved personal flotation devices, oars, bailing buckets, and running lights at night are required. Children under 12 are encouraged to wear flotation devices at all times on the water because lake water temperatures are so cold. Even if you wear a personal flotation device, you can perish from hypothermia—critical loss of body heat—if you are not rescued soon after immersion. The water is cold. (For hypothermia information please see Backcountry Basics.)

Write to the park for a list of applicable boating regulations.

Skagit Tours For half a century the Seattle City Light utility has been operating tours of its Skagit Power Project for the public. The tours will take you to the generating facilities and let you cruise Diablo Lake and ride the incline railway. Tours include a meal and slide presentation. For information and reservations write: Seattle City Light Skagit Tour Desk, 1015 Third Avenue, Seattle, WA 98104, or phone (206) 625-3030. You can stop in at the tour office in Diablo, but tours are often booked several days ahead. To book a specific day on your vacation itinerary, make a reservation some weeks ahead.

River Running The fast waters of the undammed lower Skagit challenge floaters. You can launch private crafts at the Goodell launch site beside the Goodell Campground. River-running permits (required) and a list of rules governing this sport are available at the Marblemount Ranger Station (see map) or by writing to the park. You must have approved personal flotation devices, a bailing bucket, and a trash receptacle. Wear life preservers at all times when floating the river.

Float trips are offered by private commercial services. Write to the park for a current list of outfitters.

Accommodations

Campgrounds The three National Park Service campgrounds along Highway 20 are Goodell Creek, Newhalem Creek, and Colonial Creek. Their combined capacity is 300 sites. West of the park there are state and county campgrounds at Rockport on Highway 20. Along the Cascade River Road out of Marblemount there are two U.S. Forest Service primitive campgrounds and one Department of Natural Resources campground before you reach the Cascade Pass Trailhead. East of the park the Forest Service has four campgrounds between Washington Pass and Mazama.

Goodell Creek Campground lies on the west side of the confluence of Goodell Creek and the Skagit River. This rustic campground is suitable for tents and small trailers. Drinking water, pit toilets, and a launch area for river rafters are provided. The campground is open year round, but snow may cover the ground between December and March. During the summer season a modest fee is charged. You can walk or drive to the interpretive programs at Newhalem Creek Campground, just across the Skagit. Here you camp to the constant music of the river sequestered beneath impressive forest giants.

Newhalem Creek Campground lies along the south bank of the Skagit near its confluence with Newhalem Creek, next to the small Seattle City Light town of Newhalem. There are sites suitable for both tents and trailers, and a small number of walk-in sites. Facilities include drinking water, flush toilets, and a trailer dump station. There are no hookups. A fee is charged for overnight camping. Information services are provided, as are ranger-guided walks and talks and evening campfire programs. Short hikes and a nature trail are available nearby. Ask about longer hikes at the campground information station. From the station you can glimpse peaks of the awesome Picket Range on clear days. The campground is open from mid-June through Labor Day. The walk-in sites provide excellent opportunities to break in backcountry gear—or to break into backpacking. Several sites lie just above the river bank, so the river sounds enhance your solitude. All this lies within a short walk of your car and modern comfort facilities! There are two group camping sites nearby; for information on required reservations, write to the park. Some groceries may be purchased at the Newhalem General Store of Seattle City Light, in Newhalem.

Colonial Creek Campground lies along the Thunder Arm of Diablo Lake, with campsites on both sides of Highway 20. Most sites accommodate both trailers and tents, some just tents,

Kayakers ply the free-flowing Skagit River well downstream from Gorge Dam (middle photo). Arctic Creek Falls (bottom photo) tumbles off Ross Lake's west shore across from Desolation Peak. Ross Dam, highest and furthest upriver of the three Skagit Power Project dams, backs up Ross Lake just into Canada.

and there are walk-in sites. The campground is open mid-April through November and is usually free of snow from about May through November only. A fee is charged in summer for overnight camping. Facilities include flush toilets, piped water, a trailer dump station, boat launching ramp, and a fish cleaning station. There are no hookups. From late June through early September, nature walks and talks and campfire programs are conducted. There is a self-guiding nature trail nearby, and you can take walks or short hikes along the Thunder Creek and Panther Creek Trails. The nearest food service and light groceries are at Diablo Lake Resort.

Hozomeen Campground, a fourth vehicle-access campground in the Ross Lake portion of the park, lies at Ross Lake's north end. It is not accessible via Highway 20. You reach it by driving the gravel road 40 miles south out of Hope, British Columbia. Open from mid-May to October 31, it offers more than 100 sites, accommodating tents and trailers. Facilities include pit toilets, piped water, and boat launch ramp (after mid-June). There are no trailer hookups or dump station. Nearest gasoline is at Hope, B.C. Information and backcountry permit services are available at the entrance station. Check the schedule there or in the campground for talks and evening campfire programs. The self-guiding nature trail lies along the United States-Canada boundary, beginning just steps from the entrance station. Ask a ranger about other short walks and day-hikes nearby.

General Camping Information and Regulations A campgrounds information chart is available free. Write to the park, or ask for one at a park information station. This lists the following for the whole park: Selected facilities; activities such as fishing, hunting, and boating; and methods of access, whether by vehicle, boat, or on foot. **Supplies** Groceries, meats, and general merchandise are available at Marblemount. Limited supplies are available in Newhalem and at Diablo Resort. Plan your food supplies accordingly. **Regulations** Campfires are permitted only in the fireplaces provided by the National Park Service. Bring your own firewood; no firewood collecting is permitted in Colonial Creek, Newhalem Creek, or Goodell Creek Campgrounds. House trailers and camper pickups may not drain any refuse on the ground.

Resorts Resort services are provided in the park area along Highway 20 by Diablo Lake Resort, P.O. Box 176, Rockport, WA 98283, or call the Everett, Washington, operator (area code 206) and ask for Newhalem 5578; and by Ross Lake Resort, Rockport, WA 98283, or call the Everett, Washington, operator (area code 206) and ask for Newhalem 7735. Advance reservations and arrangements for boating and/ or fishing services are always required. Ross Lake Resort is a resort that is afloat on Ross Lake and cannot be reached by road. Diablo Lake Resort offers some winter services; call for information and rates. Check in advance before planning to use credit cards at either resort.

Nearby Accommodations Accommodations, services, and facilities are very limited along Highway 20 between Marblemount, west of the Cascades crest, and Winthrop and Twisp, east of the crest. Groceries and gasoline and food service and lodgings are few and far between. Available accommodations may be full. Plan your itinerary accordingly and make reservations well ahead of your trip.

Lake Chelan and Stehekin

Information Centers A joint U.S. Forest Service and National Park Service information center sits lakeside at 428 West Woodin Avenue in the town of **Chelan**. You also can get information before boarding the passenger boat at Fields Point, but the bustle of boarding and baggage arrangements somehow consumes pre-boarding time. At **Stehekin Landing** full information services are available at the National Park Service's **Golden West Visitor Center** and at the ranger station. The visitor center offers information, exhibits, scheduled naturalist talks and walks, evening programs, and map and publications sales. The building itself is like an exhibit recalling the famous hotel era on historic Lake Chelan. **Backcountry and Climbing Permits** and information also can be obtained at the visitor center. **For information by mail**, write to the park. Allow plenty of lead time if you need specific advice about backcountry travel.

Getting to Stehekin Landing There is no road access to Stehekin Landing, which leaves you three options: boat, fly, or walk. Most people choose the first option, relying on the passenger ferry. One of the boarding points— with ample parking—for the uplake ferry is at Fields Point, about 16 miles from the town of Chelan on the lake's south shore. There is boarding at Chelan, too, where the ferry begins and ends her trips. For boating schedules and rates information write or call the Lake Chelan Boat Company, P.O. Box 186, Chelan, WA 98816, (509) 682-2224. To fly in, write or call

Harry Buckner describes life on his former family farm, now the Buckner place at Stehekin, in the Lake Chelan National Recreation Area. Backpackers make camp (middle photo) much higher up the valley. Winter turns the lower Stehekin Valley into ideal country for snowshoeing and crosscountry skiing.

Chelan Airways, P.O. Box W, Chelan, WA 98816, (509) 682-5555, or 682-5065. You can travel by private craft—the distance all the way up the lake is some 50 miles—but this requires experience and preparation. Lake Chelan's waters can be hazardous to small craft, and sudden, strong winds can pose further safety hazards. Hiking in is possible, but it involves backpacking. The most direct route is over Cascade Pass (see map) from the Cascade River Road off Highway 20 at Marblemount. There are other, generally longer and equally arduous, backpacking options. Write to the park for further information.

Naturalist Programs Naturalist programs are scheduled to help you make the most of your time here, whether you come by ferry for the day, or plan to stay over one or more nights. **If you come for the day only**, you can take a walk with a park ranger and still have time for lunch before the ferry returns to Chelan. Check at the Golden West Visitor Center as soon as you arrive. This provides a good chance to "walk off" your long ferry ride and to get glimpses of the lake and the Cascade Range from some elevation near the visitor center. If you stay overnight, further options are open. **Morning Nature Walks** Two-hour morning nature walks explore natural themes, such as stream life, plant adaptations, and tree identification. A van shuttles you to the trail with your ranger guide. **Buckner Place Walk** This is a must if you want to sense the pioneering self-sufficiency of the Stehekin lifestyle that developed in the early 1900s. This two-hour, ranger-led walk explores this historic homestead and its orchard. **Evening Programs** Rangers present programs each evening in summer in the visitor center. The architecture lends itself to friendly informality and enjoyable give-and-take between the ranger and the audience. These theme explorations of Stehekin and the North Cascades vary nightly through the week, so you can get new looks at your surroundings each night of your stay here. Evening programs may occasionally include members of the Stehekin Valley community, perhaps for a square dance, talent show, or discussion of local history. **Schedules of naturalist programs** are posted at the ferry landing, in the visitor center, and in the ranger station above the post office.

Activities

Ferry Trip for the Day You should plan ahead how you will use your layover time at Stehekin if you come by ferry for the day only. A concessioner's bus will be waiting at the landing to take you to Rainbow Falls (fee). If you choose this trip, you may want to purchase a sack lunch while still on the ferry. After the Rainbow Falls trip you probably will have time to stop at the visitor center, the concession-operated shops, or the cafe. The stopover time is about an hour and a half. The key to a satisfying visit is to make plans in advance.

The following activities are options for those whose Stehekin stay amounts to the better part of a day, or longer.

Shuttle Bus System The shuttle buses that ply the valley road are operated by the National Park Service and may be used by backpackers, day hikers, anglers, lodge guests—by all Stehekin visitors. Schedules are posted at the landing, visitor center, ranger station, and at each campsite along the Stehekin valley road. Weather and road conditions permitting, the shuttle buses run between the landing and Cottonwood Camp (see map), at the Cascade Pass Trailhead. There are other trail connections at Rainbow Falls, High Bridge, Bridge Creek, and Flat Creek. These include the Pacific Crest Trail. The options for backpackers are manifold. There are also options for day hikers. Ask about them at the visitor center or ranger station. If you are interested in fishing, the shuttle bus can put you within walking distance of good waters, including lakes, the Stehekin River, and tributary streams. If you merely want to see the valley, go along for the ride, but the continuous trip can be grueling. The road is rough and the going is slow once you leave the initial, short stretch of pavement. Modest fees are charged by zones for this unique service.

Day Hiking in Stehekin Nine hikes of a day or less are listed in the free brochure, "Day Hiking in Stehekin." Write to the park for a copy, or pick one up at the ranger station or visitor center. You can take the relatively level Lakeshore Trail out and back in a day, or make such stiff climbs as Purple Mountain. Your rewards are exceptional views of the valley and Lake Chelan. Many of these day hikes require that you use the shuttle bus, which adds to your adventure. Please carry a shuttle bus schedule and your watch. You also will need drinking water and snacks. Take a jacket and be wary of changing weather. Stay on the trails, and remember that bears and rattlesnakes always have the right-of-way. **Note**: If you have a special interest, for example in aquatic life, photography, or wildflowers, ask for custom day-hiking advice at the ranger station or visitor center.

Exploring the Upper Valley To explore the upper valley for day hikes you must rely on the shuttle bus for transportation to and from trailheads. Wide views open up as you ascend the Stehekin Valley, spreading before you the jumbles of glacier-clad peaks that characterize the North Cascades. The many glorious subalpine meadows and rushing streams may prove the inspirations of a lifetime. You can reach Cascade Pass and climb Sahale Mountain on a day trip, or devote your time to exploring Horseshoe Basin and the ruins of the historic Black Warrior Mine. These are among trail suggestions in the free "Exploring the Upper Valley" brochure. Write to the park for a copy, or pick one up at the ranger station or visitor center. Don't overextend yourself. Carry drinking water, a first-aid kit, and extra food and clothes. Do not try to cross fords or streams in high water; they can be treacherous at these steep stream gradients. Take your time, relax, and try to sense the subtle rhythms of your surroundings. Ask at the ranger station or visitor center for customized hiking advice.

Horse Use Horseback trip and horse packing services are provided by Cascade Corrals, Stehekin, WA 98852. Write for information and rates.

Picnicking There are public picnic tables (no fires, please) close to the Stehekin Landing. Ask the nearest park ranger, or check at the visitor center or ranger station for locations and other options. Picnic supplies and some groceries are sold at the North Cascades Lodge Store. You also can purchase carryout lunch items at the lodge snack bar. Please leave your picnic site as clean or cleaner than you found it.

Boat and Bicycle Rentals Boats, mopeds, and bicycles may be rented at the North Cascades Lodge. All federal boating regulations apply on Lake Chelan. You may examine a copy of the regulations at the ranger station or visitor center, or write ahead to the park for a free copy. Bicycling is best confined to the paved portion of the valley road, the lower 4 miles. Bicycling to Rainbow Falls can be pleasant and enjoyable.

River Running Float trips operate from time to time on the Stehekin River. Write to the park for up-to-date information.

Winter Activities The North Cascades Lodge and a few private valley accommodations provide winter services. Cascade Corrals (see Horse Use, above) leads ski trips in winter. The valley makes excellent cross-country skiing terrain and takes on a completely different, even quieter character in winter. Write to the park for information on winter activities and special winter safety considerations. The Lake Chelan Boat Company operates the passenger ferry on a reduced schedule in winter.

Accommodations

Camping There are no large, vehicle access campgrounds in Stehekin, for obvious reasons: you can't get there by car. The campgrounds are designed with the assumption that you have carried your gear here on your back and in your hands. There are no trailer hookups or dump stations, no laundry, shower, and sink comfort stations. A 22-site boat-access campground is at Weaver Point, across the lake from the Stehekin Landing. It is a 3.5-mile hike from there to the shuttle bus connection at Harlequin Campground (see map). Camping at Stehekin Landing is limited to five sites at the Purple Point Campground. These are often occupied by backpackers—including Pacific Crest Trail through-hikers—laying over for ferry connections or awaiting supplies via ferry or the Stehekin post office. **You cannot reserve sites**, so you can't be sure of being close to Stehekin's shops.

What may look like a disadvantage is, however, an unusual opportunity. At Stehekin you can get off the ferry, get on a shuttle bus, and go to one of the numerous campgrounds along the valley road (see map). Here you enjoy virtual backcountry camping—without carrying your gear great distances. This can be great for novices, young families, and seniors. *All camping at Stehekin requires a free backcountry use permit, which can be obtained at the Golden West Visitor Center.* The only exception to this is the boat-access campground at Weaver Point. (See Backcountry Basics, below, for general information about permits.)

Black bears roam freely; select your gear accordingly. Coolers will not fit in the bear-proof food caches provided at many of the campgrounds served by shuttle bus.

Group Campsites Groups may make advance reservations for camp-sites at Harlequin and Bridge Creek.

Showers and Laundry Public coin-operated shower and laundry facilities at Stehekin Landing are open in summer.

Resort Resort services are provided by North Cascades Lodge, Box W, Chelan, WA 98816 or P.O. Box 275, Stehekin, WA 98852, telephone (509) 682-4711. Advance reservations are a must in summer. The lodge offers both rooms and housekeeping units. Other services include boat and bicycle rentals, gasoline and oil, limited groceries, and novelties. The lodge is open year round. Some major credit cards, and

The Pacific Northwest: A Recreation Wonderland

Majestic Mt. Baker, at 10,775 feet elevation, crowns the Mount Baker-Snoqualmie National Forest. Here (pages 102-103) its reflection graces the surface of a small mountain lake, or tarn, in the national park's north unit. This national forest lying west and south of the park is but one of several U.S. and Canadian public land areas that surround the park. National park lands protect some 1.2 million acres of the Cascade Range. National forests protect another 14 million acres. Some forest lands surrounding the North Cascades National Park Service Complex enjoy added protection within the National Wilderness Preservation System. To the north the complex abuts British Columbia's Manning Provincial Park and Skagit Valley Recreation Area. The mass and mix of accessible public land areas combine to make this portion of the Pacific Northwest the nation's premier outdoor recreation region.

personal checks, are accepted. Please check in advance.

Other Valley Accommodations Limited accommodations are available at a few other points in the lower valley. Write to the park for information.

Fishing and Hunting

Rivers and streams, alpine lakes, and deep lakes and reservoirs—the North Cascades provide anglers all these fishing opportunities. **The Skagit River** offers rainbow and Dolly Varden trout, and annual runs of salmon, accompanied by cutthroat trout and white fish. Salmon include the silver (kokanee), humpy (pink), dog (chum), and king (chinook), but no salmon fishing is allowed on the Skagit inside the Ross Lake National Recreation area. Steelhead are sea-run rainbow trout that may weigh up to 30 pounds. A portion of the Skagit downriver from the park's west boundary is protected as a bald eagle sanctuary. Here bald eagles congregate in winter to feast on the spawning salmon. **The Stehekin River** offers anglers a good chance at rainbow and cutthroat trout. **Streams** in both the Skagit and Stehekin Districts offer trout angling that varies seasonally and with local conditions. Ask the nearest ranger for advice and current conditions. **Alpine lakes** abound in the park. Many support rainbow, cutthroat, golden, and brook trout. Most alpine lakes are accessible only by hiking or by backpacking (backcountry use permit required, see Backcountry Basics, below). **Diablo** and **Ross Lakes** offer rainbow, brook, cutthroat, and Dolly Varden trout. Please respect the closures of tributary streams on Ross Lake. These no-fishing areas protect spawning native trout populations. **Lake Chelan** offers kokanee salmon, rainbow and cutthroat trout, freshwater cod (burbot), and chinook salmon. In these large lakes and reservoirs, trolling is a popular method. Your luck will vary with time of year and local conditions. The North Cascades and the park are surrounded by fine fishing waters, including the Entiat, Methow, Fraser,and Columbia Rivers and their tributary waters.

Fishing Regulations All fishing in and around the park requires a valid Washington State fishing license, and all Washington Department of Game regulations, seasons, and catch limits apply. Copies of the regulations are available by mail from the Department of Game, 600 N. Capitol Way, Olympia, WA 98504. For regulations on specific fish species and specific waters in the park, ask a ranger. Fishing licenses may be obtained by mail or locally at several points in and around the park area.

Hunting Regulations Hunting is permitted in season in the Ross Lake and Lake Chelan National Recreation Areas. Hunting and the possession of any firearms are strictly prohibited in the two national park units, however. Boundaries of the national recreation areas and national park units are shown on the map appearing on pages 90-91. Hunting requires a Washington State hunting license, and all state regulations, seasons, and bag limits apply. Copies of the regulations are available by mail from the Department of Game, 600 N. Capitol Way, Olympia, WA 98504. Hunters who are in the backcountry in one of the national recreation areas overnight must obtain a backcountry use permit before setting out (see Backcountry Basics, below). Hunters using horses must follow all applicable regulations and limitations on horse use, as well as all backcountry use regulations. For answers to specific questions about hunting, write to the park.

Kokanee salmon

Dolly Varden trout

Cutthroat trout

Rainbow trout

105

Backcountry Basics

Most basic is this: If you plan to camp overnight in the backcountry, you must obtain a free backcountry use permit. A permit is required whether you are traveling afoot or by boat or on horseback. Permits may also be required in the adjacent Pasayten Wilderness Area, which is managed by the U.S. Forest Service; joint permits can be issued. Failure to comply with this requirement is a federal offense.

The permit system is designed to protect you, the quality of your backcountry experience, and the backcountry itself. With the information the permit system provides, the National Park Service can allocate backcountry use so that you are not crowded by other people during your backpacking trip. This information also enables the Park Service to monitor ecologically fragile areas and to alter use patterns to allow stressed areas to recover. The system further enables the Park Service to budget effectively for trail maintenance and backcountry management. The permit information also helps search and rescue teams know where to begin looking for you in case of emergency.

Getting a Permit Backcountry use permits are issued on a first-come, first-served basis no sooner than the day before you depart. They cannot be reserved. If you are headed for a popular backcountry destination, get your permit early in the day. This does not mean you won't get into the backcountry on a given day; but you may not get your first choice of locations. Permits can be obtained at ranger stations in Stehekin, Marblemount, and Hozomeen, and at U.S. Forest Service Ranger Stations in Early Winters, Twisp, and Glacier. Permits also can be obtained at the joint Park Service and Forest Service information station at Chelan. Permits are for specific nights at specific locations, so you need a fixed itinerary. Check for permit requirements since they may change from year to year and from agency to agency.

Local Conditions For information on local conditions—weather and trails—call the ranger stations at Chelan (509) 682-2549, or Marblemount (206) 873-4500.

Group Size The maximum number allowed in any group is 12, but the recommended party size is 5. Larger groups unavoidably have a disproportionate impact on fragile backcountry environments. **No Trailside Camping** When using maintained trails you must camp only in the camp areas that are designated with trailside posts. Cross-country camping is allowed under special conditions that will be outlined by the ranger issuing the permit.

Pets Pets are prohibited in the backcountry of the national park units. Dogs are permitted on leash in the national recreation areas and along the Pacific Crest Trail, except where otherwise posted.

Wildlife Protection Possession of firearms or other weapons is prohibited in the national park units. (See Hunting, above.) Do not feed or molest wild animals.

Horse Use Overnight backcountry horse use requires a backcountry use permit—see above. Limit your stock to the fewest possible. The maximum allowed is 15 head. Carry your feed with you; grazing is by permit only. Camp only at horse camps. For further information on horse use regulations and etiquette, ask the ranger issuing your permit, or write to the park.

Use the Wilderness Gently Reducing the impact on the backcountry helps insure that others can enjoy the wilderness, too. Please write to the park for information on minimum impact camping. Please carry and use a backpacking stove. Wood is often wet and scarce, and often its use is prohibited. When you apply for your permit, ask for a copy of all regulations, recommendations, and requests about litter, fires, and use of water sources; sanitation and waste disposal; washing yourself, dishes, and clothing; and shortcutting on switchbacks. The backcountry will remain inviting only as long as those who use it do so gently and with great wisdom.

Rescue Policy The National Park Service works with local county sheriffs and volunteer mountain rescue units. Please remember that any accident you have may also endanger the lives of those who attempt to rescue you. Good information is essential: What happened? To whom? When? Where is the victim, or where will the victim be? What equipment and human power is with the victim? What is the terrain like? What is the route into it? What are the weather and ground conditions there? Emergency numbers are: Marblemount Ranger Station (206) 873-4590; Skagit County Sheriff (206) 336-3146; Whatcom County Sheriff (206) 676-6711; and Chelan County Sheriff (509) 664-5243. Part or all of the cost of rescue operations may be charged to those who receive assistance.

Backcountry Safety Don't travel alone. Let someone know where your party is going and when to start worrying if you don't report back. Leave an emergency number to call in case you don't return. Make sure to report back when you do return. Carry extra food and survival gear. The 10 essentials are: sunglasses, knife, matches,

Mountain Climbing

A mountain climbing party (pages 108-109) skirts a crevasse on the Challenger Glacier near the summit of Mount Challenger. The North Cascades pose special challenges—and threats—to mountain climbers. Their severe, glacially-sculpted forms and omnipresent snow and ice make the climbing itself hazardous. The combination of elevation, latitude, and abundant precipitation makes weather a decisive factor in the success or failure of climbing expeditions. Exceptionally rugged terrain at the base of peaks here also makes approaching the alpine realms unusually hazardous. Because of problems of access to the heart of the range, the number and superlative quality of climbs available in the North Cascades was not fully appreciated until the 1930s and 1940s. Because many peaks have been named by climbers rather than surveyors, there is an abundance of such epithets as Formidable, Damnation, Fury, Terror, and Challenger. Climbing and backcountry use permits are coordinated at the Marblemount Ranger Station for areas accessible from Highway 20 and at Stehekin's Golden West Visitor Center for climbs accessible from Lake Chelan National Recreation Area.

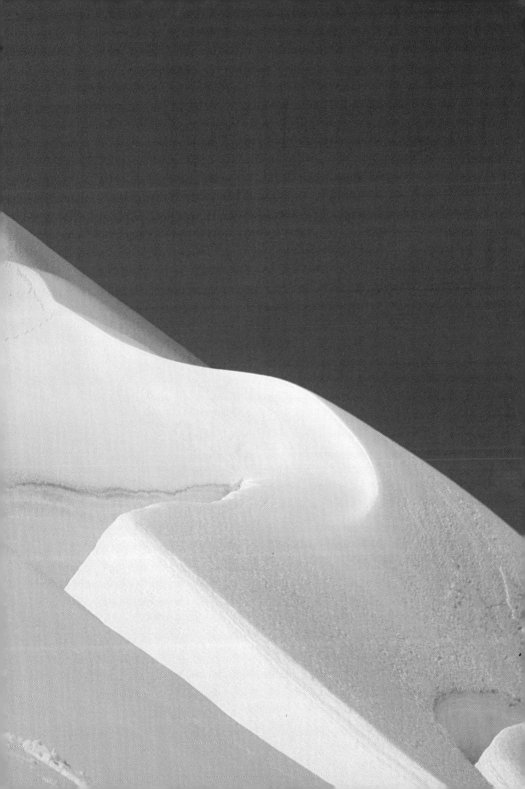

fire starter, first-aid kit, flashlight, compass, map, extra clothing, and extra food. A signaling device, such as a mirror or pen flare, can be a lifesaver. Stream crossings can be hazardous—even deadly—in spring or after heavy rains. Early morning crossings may be least hazardous. If there is any question about crossing safely, turn back. Avalanches are hazardous not only to climbers but also for hikers. If you absolutely must cross an avalanche path, do it in early morning, before 7 a.m. Have your party spread out. If someone gets caught in an avalanche, mark the spot where the person was last seen. If completely covered, a person will rarely live more than two hours, usually much less. If you are an avalanche victim, try to stay on top of the slide by making swimming motions.

Guided Trips If the backcountry attracts you, but you don't want to try it on your own, numerous outfitters serve the North Cascades area. For a list of hiking and backpacking outfitters, write to the park.

Hypothermia Hypothermia—critical loss of body heat—is an all-season killer, particularly in high-elevation areas subject to continuous wet weather. The symptoms develop fast, and the more they progress, the less capable you are of being aware of their significance. **Recognize the symptoms:** Hands and feet become numb as blood tries to supply vital organs adequately. This results in uncontrollable shivering, fumbling, and drowsiness. Without proper treatment the next stages are stupor, collapse, and death. **Avoid hypothermia** by staying dry, seeking shelter from winds, preventing exhaustion, eating lots of high-energy foods, and wearing a wool cap. The cap can help you retain up to 50 percent of the body heat which can be lost through the head and neck. **Treat hypothermia immediately.** For mild symptoms, get the victim out of the wind and rain, strip off all wet clothing. Give the victim something warm to drink, and provide dry clothes and a warm sleeping bag. If the victim is losing consciousness, skin-to-skin contact inside a dry, warm sleeping bag is the most effective treatment. Try to keep the victim awake. Hypothermia is also an immediate hazard to immersion victims in the cold, deep lakes in the park. Nationwide, hypothermia takes far more human lives yearly than does any other single outdoor hazard.

Bear Warnings Animals generally avoid human contacts, but they won't pass up what looks like an easy meal. Bears do not look upon an adult human as an easy meal. Avoid doing anything that changes their life patterns, or makes them associate humans with easy foodstuffs. **Follow these guidelines:** Eat all the food you cook. Store all foods in tight plastic bags. Clean up camp after meals. Wash dishes away from camp and streams. Carry out all your garbage, and any you find that others have left. Report all bear contacts to a park ranger. **If a bear comes into your camp:** Try to frighten it away by yelling at it, or by hitting pots and pans together. Do not hit the bear. If you cannot frighten the bear away, leave the area and report the incident to a park ranger. **Hang your food**: Use bear poles or cables for hanging your food wherever they are provided. Learn to hang your foodstuffs from a line between trees otherwise. Ask for instructions and a diagram when you apply for your backcountry permit. You may write to the park for a free copy of the National Park Service brochure, "Beware, Bears!" The park contains black bears. The last reliable grizzly sighting in the park was in 1965. Such occasional strays usually wander south from Canadian wilds.

Mountain Climbing

Rock and weather conditions are both severe in the North Cascades. Just getting to the peaks challenges many mountaineers. Hazards of unfamiliarity confront even seasoned climbers on their first North Cascades climbs. Mountain climbing here requires previous experience; safe, adequate, tested equipment and gear; the best current, local information on weather and conditions that you can obtain; and good technical skill matched by caution and commonsense. Climbing guidebooks are available for the park area. Write to the park for further information. Please remember that all overnight climbing trips require that you get a backcountry use permit (see above). The Marblemount Ranger Station is the backcountry and climbing information station for the Skagit District. The Golden West Visitor Center provides backcountry and climbing information for the Stehekin District.

Management Concerns and Safety

Even at low elevations in the park the terrain can be steep, mosses slippery, rock loose, and the weather subject to sudden changes. Stay on trails where possible, wear sturdy, non-slip footgear, and don't overtax your physical limits.

The waters are too cold for safe swimming. The rivers and streams are fast, and, therefore, dangerous. Be careful in crossing rushing streams without bridges. Lake waters are cold and often deep right off the shoreline.

Do not leave young children unattended near park waters.

Steep and winding roads make driving unusually hazardous. So does the stupendous scenery. Pull off the road at overlooks and other areas provided for scenery gazing and rest stops. Drive defensively; the other driver may be under the influence of scenery, too.

Do not feed, handle, or injure wildlife.

Know the safety aspects of any activity you undertake, or ask advice of a park ranger before you set out. For the most part, once you leave your car or boat here, you are on your own in the wilderness.

Do not drink from unapproved water sources without first boiling the water vigorously for at least one full minute. All untreated waters must be considered potential carriers of *Giardia lamblia,* protozoa that cause "backpacker's diarrhea." Symptoms may not show up until weeks after you drink contaminated water.

Should you become lost, stay where you are, find shelter, mark your location so it can be seen from the air, and wait. If the park staff knows you are missing or overdue, a search will start soon. Most lost people find that being patient is the hardest part of their experience.

Index to Activities, Services, and Facilities

☆GPO:1985—461-442/20004